50 YEARS OF HIP-HOP BU$INE$$

RECLAIMING THE BEAT
The Journey from Exploitation to Empowerment

ASH CASH

All rights reserved under the international and Pan-American copyright conventions.

First published in the United States of America.

All rights reserved. With the exception of brief quotations in a review, no part of this book may be reproduced or transmitted, in any form, or by any means, electronic or mechanical (including photocopying), nor may it be stored in any information storage and retrieval system without written permission from the publisher.

DISCLAIMER

The advice contained in this material might not be suitable for everyone. The author designed the information to present his opinion about the subject matter. The reader must carefully investigate all aspects of any business decision before committing to him or herself. The author obtained the information contained herein from sources he believes to be reliable and from his own personal experience, but he neither implies nor intends any guarantee of accuracy. The author is not in the business of giving legal, accounting, or any other type of professional advice. Should the reader need such advice, he or she must seek services from a competent professional. The author particularly disclaims any liability, loss, or risk taken by individuals who directly or indirectly act on the information contained herein. The author believes the advice presented here is sound, but readers cannot hold him responsible for either the actions they take, or the risk taken by individuals who directly or indirectly act on the information contained herein.

Published by 1BrickPublishing
Printed in the United States
Copyright © 2024 by Ash'Cash
ISBN 978-1949303506

DEDICATION

As you embark on the captivating journey through hip-hop's history, from its exploitative origins to its empowering impact, I want to express my deepest gratitude for your interest in this book. This work is dedicated to all those who recognize the transformative power of hip-hop culture and its profound influence on communities, industries, and lives.

Let this book serve as a guiding light of knowledge and inspiration for those seeking a deeper understanding of the evolution of hip-hop business over the past 50 years. May the insights and revelations within these pages equip you with the wisdom and resilience to navigate the complexities of the industry.

Prepare to be inspired by stories of resilience, innovation, and empowerment that lie ahead. Together, let us reclaim our own rhythm and stride towards abundance and prosperity.

DEDICATION REQUEST

Please share this book with anyone who seeks to understand the journey of hip-hop business over the past 50 years and how we can reclaim its power for the future.

TABLE OF CONTENTS

Introduction: From Beats to Billions 1

Part I: Exploitation 7
Chapter 1: The Early Days - Unfair Record Deals 9

Chapter 2: The Rise of 360 Deals and Loss of Control 25

Chapter 3: Going from Artist to Icon - When
Business Gets Personal. 37

Part II: Empowerment 55
Chapter 4: Following the Money - Understanding
Hip-Hop Economics 57

Chapter 5: Beyond the Hype - Building
Sustainable Hip-Hop Ventures 85

Chapter 6: Betting on Yourself - Hip-Hop Career
Strategy Breakdowns. 107

Part III: The Future 131
Chapter 7: Web3, Crypto, and New Frontiers 133

Chapter 8: Global Reach and Cultural Impact 147

Chapter 9: Keeping the Beat - Sustaining Hip-Hop's Legacy 157

Part IV: Building Wealth 175
Chapter 10: Charting YOUR Blueprint - Defining the Vision. 177

Chapter 11: Securing Your Squad - Building the Team 199

Chapter 12: Own Your Path - Launching the Venture. 211

Conclusion: The Beat Goes On. 223

About the Author 237

INTRODUCTION

FROM BEATS TO BILLIONS

In 1973, DJ Kool Herc, also known as the "Founder of Hip-Hop," kicked off a series of back-to-school parties in the rec room of his apartment building on Sedgwick Avenue in the Bronx. Little did he know, these parties would give birth to a massive global sub-culture and industry worth billions of dollars. This influential movement has impacted music, art, fashion, and business like nothing else before.

In just 50 years, hip-hop has risen from its humble and raw beginnings to become a force to be reckoned with in the music and entertainment industry. Its influence spans from the streets of Manhattan to the fashion-forward hubs of Milan, from gritty urban corners to suburban shopping malls. With each passing year, hip-hop tightens its grip on the charts and captures the attention of our collective cultural consciousness.

Now, there's no denying that hip-hop is the powerhouse of American mainstream music. The 2021 year-end report by MRC Data and Billboard reveals an unprecedented milestone: hip-hop/R&B has emerged as the dominant genre in the U.S. when it comes to overall music consumption. According to the report, "R&B/hip-hop remained the most popular genre in the U.S. in 2021, accounting for 33.5 percent of total album equivalent unit consumption and 34.7 percent of total on-demand song streams."

Both the numbers and our shared awareness confirm what we already know: Hip-Hop culture has not only made its mark, but it also propels creativity and commercial success across the global music landscape.

Hip-hop has shaped more than just the music industry - it has sparked a thriving business ecosystem. Starting in the late 1980s, when mainstream record labels embraced hip-hop, it opened doors for wider distribution. This increased visibility led to commercial success for artists and expanded their business ventures beyond album sales.

Over the decades, the hip-hop scene has fostered diverse entrepreneurial opportunities. Pioneers like Russell Simmons' Phat Farm paved the way for fashion lines in the 90s. In the 2000s, Master P and Queen Latifah secured TV production deals, and Jay-Z now leads company acquisitions and investment syndicates. Hip-hop moguls have also explored countless other creative avenues to monetize their success, including fashion, film, TV, tech, and even alcohol.

From Grandmaster Flash to 50 Cent, Dr. Dre to Sean "Diddy" Combs, the hip-hop space has given rise to some of music history's most influential artist-entrepreneurs. They have not only produced hit records but also leveraged their creativity to build empires in various industries.

Hip-hop revolutionized the game by being the first to blend entertainment and entrepreneurship, paving the way for artists to make big money moves. With iconic music careers and successful businesses, hip-hop artists showed the world what a recording artist could really achieve. And it's not just in music - actors, models, and public figures have followed suit, using their fame to launch their own companies. But it was hip-hop that set the trend, inspiring others like Jessica Simpson and Rihanna to step outside their creative careers and find business success. Unlike any other genre, hip-hop embraced the hustle and pursued innovation to grow their pockets and their empires at the same time.

The hip-hop business landscape has come a long way, but let's not forget its rough beginnings. Socio-economic inequality and exploitation have been underlying issues in hip-hop's history. Although hip-hop has achieved commercial success today, it was largely built on the backs of black and brown artists who were not given fair treatment early on. Just as inner city youth used music to escape poverty, the business side of hip-hop resulted in music executives accumulating wealth while artists struggled financially, despite their public success. Hip-hop's story is one of overcoming adversity, creatively and commercially.

Hip-hop, at its 50-year milestone, finds itself at a crucial turning point. Its influence is growing, but so are the disparities within the culture. Today's hip-hop artists have more potential for making money than ever before, with a wide range of business opportunities at their fingertips. However, the sad truth is that much of the commercial success in hip-hop has ended up in the hands of corporate entities, rather than the artists themselves. Despite being used to sell products and services worldwide, hip-hop has not translated into financial freedom or generational wealth for most of its creators. This is why "50 Years of Hip-Hop Business" is a significant moment for reflection and an chance for change. It's time for hip-hop artists to take back control over their art and the ways they profit from it. After decades of exploitation, it's finally time for empowerment.

This book is all about shifting the focus of hip-hop culture from exploitation to empowerment. It takes us on a thrilling journey through the past fifty years of the art and business of hip-hop, set to the rhythm of the beats we all love. By delving into history, we can learn from mistakes and pave the way for a better future. "50 Years of Hip-Hop Business" dives into the game-changing moments in hip-hop's commercial trajectory. It uncovers the deals that have shaped the industry, both for the better and the worse. Plus, it explores the fascinating dynamics between culture and commerce, laying bare the economics and ethics involved. Get ready to gain insights and perspective like never before.

The first part of this book reflects on how artists have been taken advantage of through predatory practices. It then offers a guidebook for empowerment in the second half. Instead of just criticizing the current state of the hip-hop industry, this book provides solutions and ideas for creating a fairer and more prosperous ecosystem. It explores the barriers that have prevented hip-hop icons from building wealth and passing it on to future generations. It's a call to action to change direction and pave the way for a better future in hip-hop.

Correcting decades of commercial distortion won't be easy, but don't underestimate hip-hop's resilience, conscience, and innovative spirit. What started as a genre from society's margins has taken center stage, dominating both the charts and culture. And despite past predatory practices, hip-hop has birthed billion-dollar companies and global celebrities. Now, imagine the possibilities if that entrepreneurial energy is fully unleashed with fair business practices. In the second half of this book, we lay out a paradigm where hip-hop's underdogs become unstoppable, taking charge of their own destinies.

Imagine a future where hip-hop's impact is not only felt through its music but also through its economic influence. Hip-hop artists and creators should have ownership over their own success, not just be token figures in someone else's empire. It is time for the architects of this culture to own their own houses, both figuratively and literally. I envision a day where hip-hop becomes a force for community-focused entrepreneurship, providing financial stability for its pioneers and current leaders. Hip-hop deserves more than just recognition in museums; it deserves to be a vehicle for generational wealth. "50 Years of Hip-Hop Business" sheds light on this need and sets a new path forward. Let this be the roadmap that transforms hip-hop from exploitation to empowerment after 50 incredible years.

Join us on a transformative journey as we explore the history of hip-hop and pave the way for a brighter future. In Part 1, we dive into the challenges artists faced in achieving financial freedom, despite the industry's commercial success. Uncover the hidden truths behind crooked contracts and the loss of wealth by hip-hop icons' heirs. In Part 2, we present innovative solutions to overcome these obstacles, empowering hip-hoppreneurs through education, ownership, and community building. Part 3 delves into the exciting technological and social trends that will shape the next 50 years of hip-hop, ensuring financial growth and ethical practices. Finally, in Part 4, we provide a concrete roadmap to harness the power of hip-hop for personal and community wealth. By the end of this journey, we aim to leave you informed, inspired, and ready to create a new business paradigm that empowers artistic entrepreneurs in the hip-hop world.

PART I: EXPLOITATION

CHAPTER 1

THE EARLY DAYS - UNFAIR RECORD DEALS

Before hip-hop artists dominated the business world with their own brands, they had to fight against corporate systems for respect and fair compensation in the music industry. The path to success in hip-hop has always been an uphill battle, with early pioneers often facing unjust record deals in order to have their music distributed by major labels. The tension between fair treatment for hip-hop artists and the desire of record labels and executives to make money off their talent began early in the genre's rise to commercial success. To understand how Hip-Hop Icons were cheated while labels profited, you must understand Industry rule #4080, which, in the immortal words of A Tribe Called Quest's Q-Tip, "Record company people are shady."

The 1970s through mid-1980s were a pivotal time for hip-hop, filled with talented DJs and MCs who revolutionized the genre. However, there was a major hurdle - there was no established way to commercially package and sell this music. This meant that the incredible talent showcased at block parties in the Bronx couldn't easily reach a larger audience. The connection between creative work and consumer markets had not yet been established in the industry, so early deals for rappers and DJs were driven by opportunistic music entrepreneurs rather than a streamlined system to bring hip-hop to the masses.

According to legendary hip-hop journalist, author and filmmaker Nelson George, "Rappers struggled through most of the 1980s to get record deals. Major labels dismissed hip-hop as a fad not worth their time." However, this didn't stop the genre from gaining popularity on the streets. It wasn't until groundbreaking albums like NWA's Straight Outta Compton and Public Enemy's It Takes A Nation of Millions came out that hip-hop finally caught the attention of the mainstream. These projects offered raw and honest commentary on urban life, pushing boundaries both musically and socially.

Major record labels finally caught on to the success of these albums, which were gaining momentum and popularity in the world of hip-hop. But instead of embracing the unique cultural force behind its rise, they stuck to their old-fashioned pop music deals. This limited the artistic potential of hip-hop, as it was forced into outdated contracts designed for pop stars rather than allowing it to thrive as a force of cultural empowerment. Hip-hop broke all the rules about what sells in popular music, but the labels held it back with their rigid ways.

In the late 80s and 90s, as hip-hop acts were getting signed to major labels, their contracts started resembling those of pop, rock, and R&B artists. These deals would lock artists into lengthy partnerships with the labels, spanning an average of 5-7 albums over a decade. Artists would receive upfront advances of a few hundred thousand dollars but would have to repay the label by giving up a large percentage of their record sales revenue before earning royalties.

While a $500,000 advance may seem like a significant amount for a new artist, it didn't fully capture the massive commercial potential of hip-hop during that time. Unfortunately, these advances came at the cost of complicated legal language and financial obligations that many artists didn't fully understand at the beginning of their careers.

Researchers Carl W. Battle and Michael Bennett have highlighted the imbalanced power dynamic between hip hop artists and record labels in their study on rap music contracts. In the early days, record labels had the upper hand, using their leverage to negotiate highly favorable terms. However, as rap music grew in popularity during the 1990s and early 2000s, the balance of power began to shift. It took some time for the equilibrium to be reached, as record labels took advantage of outdated contract clauses despite the increasing dominance of hip-hop as a revenue driver for the mainstream.

Hip-hop sales generated billions for record labels while artists and their families struggled to make a living. According to statistics offered by The History of Record Labels and the Music Industry, from the mid-80s to the 90s, "rap and hip-hop accounted for nearly $2.4 billion in record sales" in the U.S. alone. Nelson George pointed out "major labels were generating more than $700 million annually off of hip-hop music sales" by the early 1990s, seizing eagerly on rap's commercial breakthrough.

Despite these numbers, multi-platinum hip-hop acts of the late 80s and 90s era like MC Hammer, TLC, Snoop Dogg and Wu Tang Clan faced bankruptcies, debt and legal troubles despite moving millions of albums for labels. "Record companies made tens of millions off of Tupac's albums alone, yet his mother's home was in foreclosure at the time of his death and Tupac's estate was bankrupt when he died" notes media analyst Zack

O'Malley Greenburg. The obvious disparity between corporate gains and the struggles faced by artists brings to light the unjust realities of the early hip-hop era.

The obstacles that held back hip-hop artists from making money off their talent, despite its growing impact on global culture, can be attributed to these various factors:

1. Album Sales Revenue Structure: Hip-hop albums were regularly among the top sellers annually, moving hundreds of thousands and even millions of units. But here's the catch - artists were only getting a measly 12-20% royalty rates on albums based on outdated industry norms, requiring them to reach astronomical multi-platinum certification levels just to see some serious cash flow after recovering their expenses and advances. This meant that hip hop artists had to pull off sales miracles to be fairly compensated for the impact their music had on our culture

2. The Shift in the Ringtone Era: As digital music platforms like Napster, iTunes, and streaming services emerged, the popularity of physical album sales started to decline. This posed a challenge for hip-hop artists who relied on album sales for income, as the new digital consumption models were still in the early stages of monetization. At the same time, record labels were making millions off of hip-hop artists' hit songs through ringtone sales. Unfortunately, artists struggled to find a compensation model that matched the income they had previously earned from album sales.

3. The Labels' Grip on Touring & Merchandise Revenue: Labels found a way to secure additional revenue by leveraging the success of artists' live tours and merchandise. Through their contracts, labels made sure they received a share of the income generated from touring, publishing, and merchandising. This arrangement left artists with limited direct earnings from their devoted fanbase who attended shows and purchase merchandise.

Hip-hop icons of the 1990s faced financial struggles despite their cultural impact. Major label deals and multi-platinum albums didn't guarantee stability. Even big sales numbers didn't translate into fair compensation. The lack of proper infrastructure left artists fighting to stay financially secure. For example, iconic conscious hip-hop duo Eric B. & Rakim faced financial disputes, which caused them to split in 1993, even while being wildly popular and successful in the eyes of their fans. Rakim explained in an interview years later, "We made a lot of money but we didn't get a lot of money. It looks good on paper, but when it was time to get checks, everything was a problem. We'd have $1,000 a night riders, stuff like that, but couldn't put any money in our pocket." The pursuit of earning what they deserved remained a challenge for hip-hop pioneers.

The music industry was rigged in favor of corporate middlemen, leaving creative talents fighting for what they deserved. One particular case that made waves in the early 1990s is NWA's clash with their label, Ruthless Records. This public contract dispute not only shed light on the unequal treatment of hip-hop artists, but also exposed the underlying racial injustices within the entertainment industry. It is clear that the lingering effects of America's troubled history with race had influenced the turbulent business beginnings of hip-hop.

NWA were the pioneers of gangsta rap who changed America. In the late 80s, this group of trailblazers emerged from Compton, California, reshaping the rap scene as we know it. Dr. Dre, Ice Cube, Eazy-E, and other talents joined forces to create NWA.

Their album, "Straight Outta Compton," completely revolutionized the culture. It boldly addressed crime, policing, and the struggles of inner-city life, all while showcasing their unrivaled DJ skills and rhythmic mastery.

Despite minimal radio play due to explicit, controversial lyrical content, the album skyrocketed to platinum status in 1988. However, the members of NWA themselves did not reap the financial rewards they deserved. Ruthless Records, their parent label, and national distribution partners exploited their groundbreaking creativity, leaving the artists with only a fraction of the revenues.

Financial tensions within NWA reached a breaking point when Ice Cube, a vital member of the group, decided to leave both the group and Ruthless Records in 1990 due to contract disputes. His manager spoke out, stating "We couldn't get a fair deal. They kept offering us these ridiculous contracts. It was like a joke…" Instead of remaining passive while white music executives profited from NWA's success without properly compensating the group, Ice Cube took a bold step towards independence and ownership. He hoped to change the situation and directly earn income from his own contributions and fanbase. This decision paid off immensely with the release of his solo album AmeriKKKa's Most Wanted, which went platinum. This success demonstrated that creativity should not be hindered by financial injustice.

Meanwhile, his NWA colleagues Dr. Dre and Eazy-E remained tied to Ruthless Records, the label they co-founded. Despite the incredible success of their multi-platinum NWA projects, which generated over $100 million in revenue, the artists struggled to make ends meet due to confusing contract terms and money owed to the label. Executives took advantage of their ownership protections, leaving the artists frustrated and financially strained. Desperate for a solution, Dr. Dre sought help from renowned music attorney Ed McPherson to investigate Ruthless Records' questionable practices that were draining NWA of their earnings.

During his investigation, McPherson made a shocking discovery. Distributor Priority Records had a major advantage over parent label Ruthless when it came to royalty payments. Court records showed that Priority paid Ruthless a 50% rate for each cassette and CD album sold, while the actual artists, like Dr. Dre, who created the music, received a measly 6-7% royalty. Imagine this: for every $100 in sales on an NWA album, the artists themselves were only pocketing less than $10. It's clear that the talented individuals behind this groundbreaking music were getting a mere fraction of what they deserved. This unfair and borderline criminal financial arrangement was made possible by complicated contracts between hip-hop's early power players and the artists. It's not just a disadvantage; it's outright theft.

Dr. Dre publicly expressed his frustration about not being properly compensated for his creative genius. Despite producing three successful albums for Ruthless Records, he claims that he and his fellow artists had not received fair compensation for their hard work. Dr. Dre specifically mentioned his involvement in producing Straight Outta Compton, which has sold over 4 million records, yet he only received $75,000 for his efforts. This highlights the financial discrepancies and injustice that have plagued the hip-hop industry since its early days. Additionally, the racial undertones cannot be ignored, as young black artists are being denied equity while the white music industry establishment profits from their talent.

Dre eventually left Ruthless Records, but reached a settlement that gave him ownership of his future solo projects. His album, The Chronic, became incredibly successful and introduced Snoop Dogg and G-Funk to the mainstream. Even Easy-E, who played a crucial role in creating NWA and co-founding Ruthless, faced struggles. Despite penning the original deal and discovering talented individuals like Dr. Dre, Easy-E failed to gain lasting personal leverage or financial freedom before his untimely death.

In 1995, Eazy tragically passed away from HIV/AIDS-related health complications. Despite his fame during NWA's peak years, his total assets at the time of his death amounted to just $30,000 in personal bank accounts and anticipated royalty earnings for that year. In the final 18 months of his life, Eazy struggled to make ends meet, relying on advances from Ruthless Records while his lawyers held control over his finances and rights ownership. Meanwhile, Ruthless Records continued to profit from NWA's catalog, which was built on Eazy's vision. Unfortunately, Eazy's untimely death at age 31 meant he never experienced the financial stability he deserved for his significant contributions to the genre, while his label partners retained all control and financial success.

Eazy E and Tupac Shakur, two legendary figures in hip-hop, faced similar financial struggles despite their fame. While both artists produced platinum albums and spoke out against racial injustice, their actual cash flow was surprisingly low. Music lawyer L. Londell McMillan reveals that Tupac's liquid assets were barely six figures. Despite their success, Eazy and Pac were stuck living from album to album, relying on advances. Meanwhile, corporate entities profited from their music catalogs, which were estimated to be worth around $40 million at the time of Tupac's death. The true owners of their creative work were left empty-handed, while others profited from their talent. From Wall Street to Hollywood, many benefited from Eazy and Pac's artistry, leaving the two hip-hop pioneers without the financial security they deserved.

The common theme among these two legends is that they were taken advantage of by the industry they worked with in an attempt to bring their creative talents to the commercial market. Whether it was dealing with independent agents like Jerry Heller or major record labels like Universal Music, hip-hop pioneers became risky investments for venture capitalists seeking big profits at the expense of the artists themselves. These investors used old-fashioned formulas based on outdated assumptions about what sells, completely ignoring the reality of hip-hop. The artists were forced to give up control of their work to profit-driven entities that had no real connection to the urban communities that birthed hip-hop. This power dynamic allowed music executives to exploit cultural movements and become rich without any accountability, while the artists themselves were left financially constrained. Instead of inviting the hip-hop community to share in the wealth they created, this structure held them back.

A closer look at the financial conflicts of interest reveals how mainstream players in the music industry invested very little, if at all, into the development of emerging hip-hop acts. However, once these acts started gaining popularity, these players sought to exploit their reach for profit, taking advantage of unfair ownership clauses.

Renowned music critic John Nova Lomax points out that major record companies have always treated hip-hop as a cash cow. Instead of supporting its growth and spreading it to a wider audience, they focused solely on distribution. By exclusively targeting hip-hop for radio airplay, these labels aimed to turn street credibility into sales without investing in building a sustainable foundation.

In the early stages, labels ignored the cultural significance of hip-hop, but later on, they tried to maximize its commercial potential without considering the ethical implications. This resulted in artists being tied to recording contracts that limited their creativity and made them mere commodities for production. Meanwhile, lawyers and executives overseeing these contracts positioned themselves as the primary beneficiaries, prioritizing their own interests over the artists' careers.

Hip-hop artists and producers were cheated out of their rightful share of the profits from their albums. Despite being partial owners and shaping the raw materials of hip-hop culture, they were burdened with debt under unfair contracts. Advances provided by labels were used to cover project funding costs, but it tied artists to the label for years, with no guarantee of earning a profit from their own work. Labels took advantage of outdated contract clauses to limit artist earnings, from never-ending recouping of expenses to restrictions on creative contributions. The labels had control over the artists' master recordings, allowing them to profit from various revenue streams like touring and merchandising, beyond just record sales. This legal structure deprived hip-hop acts of independent revenue options and allowed major labels to dominate the industry. They exploited the cultural movement of hip-hop, building empires at the expense of the artists.

NWA's contract crisis with Ruthless Records exposed a major problem in the hip-hop industry. These contracts allowed labels to take unfair ownership of artists' work and profits. Crafty lawyers used these imbalanced contracts to exploit black artists while appearing to comply with civil rights laws. As a result, hip-hop performers had little control over their own careers. The mainstream music industry refused to change their unfair practices, leading to a long-standing issue of exploitation in the industry.

As hip-hop evolved past the 1990s, newer artists grappled with unfair contracts and challenges when dealing with stubborn record labels that controlled major distribution. Despite the genre's immense influence on music culture, with rap now surpassing rock as the most popular genre in terms of total consumption, the financial benefits have not matched its success. Hip-hop dominates the top 40 music industry, but better financial terms have been slow to materialize.

It's been over two decades since NWA's legal rifts exposed financial discrepancies in hip-hop, shockingly, similar stories have surfaced in recent years, exposing the same unfair power dynamics and money issues affecting modern rap icons like Drake and Lil Wayne. The pattern is consistent across time and location: talented hip-hop artists work tirelessly to create culture-defining hits that make billions for media companies. However, they receive only a small fraction of the financial rewards compared to businessmen who profit from owning rights to the music.

For example, Drake's very public battle with his label, Cash Money, is reminiscent of past conflicts between artists and corporations. Despite being one of hip-hop's biggest stars, with sales comparable to Taylor Swift and Adele, Drake was denied over $19 million in royalties. The contract disputes, exposed through lawsuits filed by Drake and Lil Wayne against Birdman's label and Universal, revealed questionable accounting practices and hidden payments that prevented Drake from receiving his rightful income. To make matters worse, Forbes reported that Drake had to borrow $20 million just to gain financial freedom from Cash Money's control. This troubling situation highlights the unfairness of contracts in the music industry, where talented artists are systematically denied transparency and the payments they deserve, while middlemen profit exponentially from their hard work.

Drake's mentor, Lil Wayne, faced similar circumstances in the past. Lil Wayne, a former member of the Hot Boys, turned Cash Money Records into a successful powerhouse in the late 90s and 2000s. The label sold over 120 million albums during its peak, with Lil Wayne playing a significant role. However, in 2015, Lil Wayne filed a lawsuit against Birdman and Universal Music, claiming he was owed over $8 million in profits that he never received. Instead, he was paid below the minimum wage for his years of service. These legal battles aim to help Lil Wayne regain the financial stability that he deserves as an artist who was named Top Male Artist of the 2000s by Billboard.

The disconnect between commercial success and financial security for hip-hop stars is still prevalent, as seen in these examples. Similar to infamous stories of chart-topping groups like TLC or Five Heartbeats in past generations going bankrupt due to unfair music contracts, today we see legends like De La Soul and Teyana Taylor waging public legal fights trying to gain ownership of their classic works. Even entire sub-genres like grime and reggaeton are facing challenges when it comes to fair streaming payouts, despite driving global consumption. It's time to bridge the gap and ensure fairness in the industry.

In 2023, hip-hop finds itself at a crucial crossroads, even fifty years after its birth. Despite its huge influence on pop culture, many of the people who create hip-hop music don't have control or ownership over their work, like the rights to their songs, their original recordings, or the money they make from touring. This started with unfair contracts in the early days that gave all the power to the big music companies. Hip-hop is undeniably popular, as you can see from streaming charts and big music festivals like Coachella. But we have to recognize that there's a deep-seated unfairness in the hip-hop industry, and it still affects artists today. While artists like Kendrick,

Cardi B, and Travis Scott amass millions of plays, the system still cheats past legends like Pete Rock, Main Source, and AZ out of their rightful royalties, even decades later. It's time to address this issue and ensure fair compensation for all.

Hip-hop's commercial origins have disempowered artists for a long time, favoring certain groups and keeping past injustices status quo. The community, which has made great sacrifices to express themselves and elevate the culture globally, deserves fair compensation and an end to shady financial practices. Though the odds were initially stacked against them, there is hope for change if those within the industry step up and rewrite the rules.

Hip-hop has come a long way in the past fifty years, breaking barriers and reaching audiences worldwide. It's no longer just a nostalgic novelty, but a mainstream powerhouse that continues to evolve. The billions earned from merchandising, licensing old hits for commercials, and even creating Broadway-style movie musicals like "Beastie Boys Story" in 2022, proves there is a huge demand for hip-hop history. However, it's important to address the lack of fair business practices in the industry, and to give proper recognition to the architects who shaped this history. It's time for a much-needed reconciliation.

Lack of legal safeguards hindered hip-hop pioneers from fully enjoying their creative freedom and reaping the financial benefits of their commercial successes. Similar to blues, jazz, and rock legends of the past, rap icons were left penniless while their music thrived in the corporate world. It's time to ensure that these heroes are properly compensated in the booming Hip-Hop economy.

So, how can hip-hop evolve its business practices to make fairness a priority and support its creative community in the long term? What can we learn from past mistakes in order to seize new opportunities to ensure financial stability and empower future generations of hip-hop creators?

Some extremists argue that the only way to fix the flaws in the music industry is to completely overhaul the capitalist system that it's built upon. They believe that hip-hop, while advocating for equality and racial justice, still operates within the same societal structures that amplify the experiences of black and brown artists. However, it's important to recognize that hip-hop itself originated from capitalism, so it might be more effective to empower cultural leaders within the existing system by rewriting the rules. In pushing for change, hip-hop can challenge inequalities in the music industry and create sociopolitical progress by pressuring for reform rather than a complete demolition. Hip-hop didn't become a billion-dollar industry by avoiding mainstream platforms entirely, but by forcing them to open up opportunities for wider access.

In order for hip-hop to thrive beyond its 50th year, it must use its resilient and disruptive essence to bring about economic justice reform. Just as the lyrics of hip-hop challenged societal norms, now it's time for the business side of hip-hop to champion policy changes and shifts in power. By understanding the complexities of past exploitation and using financial knowledge as a tool for liberation, hip-hop can pave the way for a new era of prosperity. This culture has a proven track record of defying stereotypes and transforming mainstream perspectives through strategic collaboration with corporate entities. It's time to write a new empowering chapter in the world of hip-hop.

Hip-hop's future depends on breaking free from financial disparities. We see glimmers of hope, but culture keepers must keep pushing for change. The years ahead will challenge outdated music business practices, and we can't avoid tough conversations. But the potential payoff is worth it - hip-hop can break free from its past and achieve economic independence. It's time to reclaim our financial fate, starting with understanding our origins. Our journey starts now.

CHAPTER 2

THE RISE OF 360 DEALS AND LOSS OF CONTROL

As hip-hop moved into the 2000s, the music began to reflect the harsh realities of life beyond the glitz and glamour. Artists found themselves caught between systemic issues like incarceration and violence, struggling to break free. But there was a hidden trap lurking in the background - 360 deals disguised as label partnerships, robbing artists of creative control and financial freedom.

In the early 2000s, the recording industry behemoths couldn't ignore the booming popularity of hip-hop. As rock music declined, hip-hop took over the charts and dominated cultural discussions. It accounted for more than 25% of total music sales in the US during the early 2000s, reaching an astonishing 35% by the end of the decade. But little did artists know, this success came at a steep price.

Hip-hop artists like Nelly, Ja Rule, and DMX took the labels by storm, selling over 10 million albums each. But as physical sales started to decline in the digital era, music executives had to find new ways to protect their profits. This led to increased exploitation of artists as traditional sources of income became unstable.

Introducing the notorious 360 deal: a game-changing framework that goes beyond traditional recording contracts. This contract not only secures artists' album royalties but also claims a share of their touring, merchandise, endorsements, and other income streams. In fact, by 2004, a whopping 75% of major label rap/R&B agreements had embraced this all-encompassing model, keeping artists securely locked in through universal clauses.

This new structure was sold as a "partnership" between artists and the label. As the danger of online piracy grew, traditional physical sales had become less dependable. In response, record labels decided to step up their involvement to secure new sources of income for artists. This collaborative effort explored uncharted territory, aiming to create a win-win situation for everyone involved (so they said).

In reality, 360 deals were more like a corporate takeover of hip-hop talent. The music industry's 360 framework crushed the power, ownership, and transparency that artists once had. These deals, designed to maximize corporate profit, left artists with little control over their careers and brand influence.

To truly understand the negative impact of 360 deals on the world of hip-hop business, let's dive into the specific contract clauses and income sources that are affected. Through gradually tightening their grip on control beyond just album production, record labels have positioned themselves as unavoidable intermediaries, siphoning off profits from an artist's every money-making endeavor. This effectively puts musicians in a position where they have to fund their own careers by accumulating crippling debt.

Under the 360 framework, labels receive up to 30% of all touring and live performance income artists generate. They use complicated accounting tricks to deduct expenses like stage construction, rider costs, hotel expenses, per diem, and transportation before artists even see a dime. This is a big blow to artists' independence, especially since tours are their most reliable source of income in the streaming era.

In addition to that, did you know that 360 deals can snatch up to half of an artist's merchandise sales? That's right, from clothing to accessories to physical materials, labels can take a big chunk of the profits. And it's not just concert merch platforms that are affected, but also collaborations with brands. Take 50 Cent, for example. He had to shell out $4 million to Interscope, even though the label had no involvement in his vitamin water deal. Survey says... ZERO!!! (IYKYK)

The ongoing problem of imbalance in the music industry is evident in the way labels negotiate artist management deals. These deals often involve labels taking a significant percentage (30-50%) of bookings for appearances and sponsorships that have nothing to do with music, such as hosting events or promoting products. Additionally, labels have historically claimed a 20% share of the profits from artists' involvement in TV production, acting roles, literary works, or other side businesses, even though these ventures are completely separate from the label's services. By signing away their 360 rights, artists are essentially sacrificing their potential earnings from any business ventures outside of their music.

Residencies in Las Vegas have become a popular trend for hip-hop and R&B artists, but are they really just glorified tenants? Analysts like Linda Charnay argue that these semi-permanent performance engagements, along with the rise of 360 deals, strip artists of their autonomy and make them beholden to record labels.

In the ever-changing shift from physical to digital, record labels took advantage of artists by using a so-called "mutual revenue diversification" tactic. They claimed it was a win-win move for everybody, but in reality, it allowed them to unfairly control the majority of the artists' earnings. These labels convinced new hip-hop talents to trade away all their income options in exchange for upfront funding for their projects. It was a clever way for companies to exploit artists, disguising their actions as a savvy business strategy.

360 deals may have looked good on paper, but they ended up screwing over hip-hop artists financially. These deals promised a way to make up for declining album royalties by securing other sources of income. On the surface, it seemed like a good idea, with artists being offered bigger cash advances compared to standard contracts. These deals often promise bigger upfront payments, averaging around $500k, compared to the meager $180k, as reported by the Future of Music Coalition. But the reality was far from rosy.

Beneath the surface, there are serious problems in the music industry when it comes to labels taking advantage of artists and their rights. Lawyers, such as Chris Castle, have exposed the legal maneuvers that have allowed labels to gain power and profit from 360 deals without properly adapting to the digital market. These manipulative tactics, like cross-collateralization clauses, force artists to prioritize paying off debts before receiving their fair share of earnings. In the end, 360 contracts favor the business side of things rather than fostering a fair and balanced creative industry.

The financial effects on artists are devastating, hindering their progress. According to The Nation's analysis of typical 360 major label deals:

- 81% of all artist income exclusively goes toward recouping label debts rather than direct payment

- Average royalty payout equals $23.40 per $1000 in music sold vs $36.50 for album-only deals

- Median label recording budgets are $300k, requiring exceeding rare mega-hits to escape debts

While artists may have more contractual rights, 360 frameworks actually make it harder for them to recoup their expenses and earn a fair share of royalties. The numbers show that achieving mainstream success is crucial for financial security, but it's not a realistic outcome for most acts, with superstars like Jay Z and Usher being the exception rather than the rule. Estimates indicate that only the top 5% of major label signees are able to generate enough sales to receive royalty checks from common 360 deals. These contracts often require artists to slowly pay back their advances with interest before seeing any earnings.

To further expose the hidden truth behind the shiny 360 façade, a Citigroup investment report from 2015 bluntly identifies 360 deals as a scheme that gives record labels an unfair share of an artist's income without taking on the associated risks or providing adequate services. This transparent revelation exposes a business structure that prioritizes control, allowing labels to minimize their risk while maximizing their profits by burdening artists with debt and pocketing a larger portion of the revenue.

In the world of hip-hop, so-called "partnerships" have left many artists financially trapped, despite their groundbreaking contributions. These icons, known for their cultural impact and relentless touring, now face insolvency and bankruptcy. As if that weren't enough, they are also losing control over the additional income streams that once sustained their careers beyond just record sales.

Despite the obvious disadvantageous terms and unfair distribution of profits in 360 label deals, why did influential hip-hop figures like Kanye West, Usher, and Lil Wayne still choose to accept them starting from 2004?

The answer to this reveals a power imbalance, limited options, and pressure from the industry. It's hard to ignore the fact that many popular rappers started signing 360 deals right around the same time that streaming changed the music industry. But the truth is, these agreements took advantage of artists who were trying to protect themselves in the face of bigger economic changes they couldn't control.

Streaming services have significantly impacted the profitability of record labels, forcing them to find alternative ways to make up for lost revenue. As a result, many labels have turned to 360 deals, where they extract more compensation from individual artists. Music professor Erin M. Jacobson dives into the complex dynamics at play here. According to her, labels started implementing these 360 deals in the early 2000s as a response to rampant piracy, particularly with the emergence of Napster. Both artists and labels were grappling with how to make money in an era where consumers weren't paying for recorded music in the conventional way.

So, while 360 deals were sold as a way to share risk during uncertain times, the reality was that these deals became a tool for powerful corporations to take advantage of vulnerable artists. Adam Marx's analysis of the industry reveals an unbalanced system that leaves artists with no leverage. They are forced to choose between potential poverty by avoiding 360 deals or accepting overreaching terms just to get their music distributed. The days of guaranteed returns on album budgets are long gone.

Even global icons like Kanye West, known for his unique style and independence, have admitted that avoiding 360 deals becomes too challenging at a certain level of fame. Kanye reluctantly signed one himself under Universal Music's labels, acknowledging the unbalanced power dynamics that come with it. He shared, "Without a 360 deal, you feel almost insignificant. They have so much control over you that they can just shelve you...It's like either sign a 360 deal or don't release your album." This forces even the most talented individuals to submit to a system that exploits their creativity. This type of legal extortion has become the norm between mainstream hip-hop artists and labels that control physical distribution channels.

To add financial insult to contractual injury, the two largest traditional music groups Universal and Sony also control the two biggest streaming platforms respectively in Apple Music and Spotify. This allows them to reduce artist payments while making up for inflated production and video costs through contractual debt obligations. Entertainment lawyer Dina LaPolt pointed out that "the labels owning part of the streaming platform means they're making money from both the master recording ownership and platform equity." For hip-hop artists who have overcome poverty to achieve success, they are forced to choose between being exploited or losing their creative outlet.

As if being tied down by unfair label deals wasn't enough, hip-hop artists have now fallen victim to dubious accounting practices. Greedy labels are using complex methods to hide profits and line their own pockets, all at the expense of talented artists.

These labels often use confusing math to shortchange the artists. While 360 frameworks were supposed to protect artists by providing additional sources of income, this only works if there is clear and open reporting about where the money is going. Unfortunately, there are still mysterious gaps in the system that prevent many artists from seeing fair profits from their 360 deals.

The most infamous accusations of crooked accounting come from Aftermath/Interscope megastar Eminem against Universal Music. Despite selling over 250 million records worldwide and being recognized as the highest certified U.S. artist, Eminem claims he never received the proper financial statements outlining his income from 1999 to 2017. Estimates suggest that there are significant gaps in the accounting, potentially amounting to tens of millions of dollars. This discrepancy has left many bewildered, as Eminem's undeniable commercial success does not align with the lack of appropriate compensation.

Eminem's public complaints may be dismissed by some due to his fame, but the disparities between his massive record sales and the meager profits he receives are becoming increasingly obvious. His legal team claims that unethical financial practices are rampant within Universal Music Group, affecting not just hip-hop artists, but also artists from other genres. According to them, UMG uses various tactics to conceal and reduce the royalties owed to artists, and this deception is a coordinated effort that involves top-level management all the way down to subsidiary labels.

Here's the hard truth: the numbers don't lie: Universal and other big labels are pocketing huge sums of money that should be going to hip-hop artists. Forbes's investigation into music industry payouts reveals some shocking data analysis that exposes the glaring gaps in the system:

- Artists receive ~13% of total revenues the music industry generates

- Recorded music revenues globally totaled $11.2 billion in 2019 but only 12% reached artists

- Widescale "cross-collateralization" accounting tactics allow labels deducting expenses and debts disproportionately across entire artist catalogs before distributing royalties

Again, the numbers don't lie. Most of the money in hip-hop goes to the bigwigs in the music industry, while the creators who actually make the value get the short end of the stick.

From intentionally unclear accounting to questionable practices of recovering expenses, it's evident that the music industry has systematically taken advantage of artists for years. This goes beyond just a few isolated incidents - it's a persistent problem that has affected artists from Vanilla Ice to Nicki Minaj. It's clear that minor changes in industry ethics or regulations won't fix these deep-rooted imbalances overnight. However, the fact that hip-hop's biggest stars continue to face financial struggles for extended periods of time highlights the urgent need to change the way new artists engage in business.

Legal expert Cheryl Smith bluntly highlights the unbalanced nature of the 360 deal, stating, "The artist's benefits in this arrangement mainly come from the advance against their own earnings. It makes you question whether it should be called a 360 deal or a circle jerk." Her candid description emphasizes how artists surrender control over their entire business operations and receive insufficient compensation that barely covers the expenses of producing high-stakes entertainment.

Hip-Hop living legend Nas achieved immense success with six consecutive platinum albums. However, despite selling over 10 million records, he only made a measly $230k due to the intricacies of his indie and major label deals. Prodigy, one half of the acclaimed rap duo Mobb Deep, sadly passed away at just 42 years old, leaving behind a heavy debt of $500k in unpaid taxes. This highlights the struggles many artists face in trying to escape financial hardship, even with critically acclaimed works.

Lawyer Leslie T. West's research supports the notion that financial freedom is a rare occurrence for artists, particularly in the music industry. The manipulative fine print of standard recording contracts, especially under the 360 frameworks, make it even more challenging to achieve economic stability. West's analysis reveals that rappers and R&B artists face higher rates of bankruptcy and financial distress compared to rock bands, with a staggering 3-to-1 ratio. This disparity became prominent as the music industry experienced a turbulent shift from CD and ringtone sales to the era of streaming.

The reality is, behind the glitz and glamour of the music world, many artists struggle to make ends meet and endure financial challenges that are often overlooked.

Even though the media often shows rappers partying and popping champagne in clubs, this glamorous image doesn't show the real struggle that talented artists face when it comes to making money. The music industry's outdated label systems make it difficult for artists to get the compensation they deserve, even when they reach the heights of fame and critical acclaim.

The idea that talented creative geniuses who are leading a global cultural revival often struggle with their own finances and end up broke goes against all common sense. However, it is clear that throughout the history of hip-hop, unfair industry accounting practices and exploitative contracts have consistently played a major role in draining these iconic artists of their financial resources.

In 2016, there was a growing weariness of labels exerting too much control. Busta Rhymes, another hip-hop legend, shared this sentiment in interviews, revealing why he chose to independently distribute his album, Empire. Having seen fellow hip-hop artists lose control and ownership due to poor business decisions, Busta took a deliberate and innovative approach to protect his career.

Many people can relate to his rebellion, which represents a time when artists had limited options: sign away their rights or lose their independence. However, this was not a true choice. It was merely a temporary solution that prevented them from addressing the larger market changes. The good news is that the current situation allows talent to avoid being silenced creatively or suffering financially.

Forget the old ways. Streaming platforms and blockchain technology are giving artists the upper hand in their careers, sparking a revolution in ownership and compensation. With Web 3.0 at their fingertips, artists now have the tools to take back control and break free from the grip of corporate gatekeepers. No more 360 record deals holding them back if they don't want them to. It's all about collaboration and fair distribution, not monopolies. Get ready for a new era of creativity and empowerment.

the outdated infrastructure that tried to box it in, the genre is once again outshining the limitations that once held it back. Iconic hip-hop songs that once spoke of liberation from artistic oppression or financial struggles now carry even more weight as the genre itself breaks free from the corporate chains that once held it captive. No longer can artists be trapped by unfair contracts that don't serve their best interests or contribute to the larger cultural landscape. The time has come for hip-hop's pioneering spirit to redefine the rules of creative commerce.

While acknowledging the importance of acknowledging past injustices, simply dwelling on systemic problems won't get us anywhere. The beauty of hip-hop lies in its ability to break free from the confines of traditional music creation, defying expectations and embracing its fiery roots. Like DJ Kool Herc who saw the potential in the poverty-stricken streets of the Bronx in the 70s, today's hip-hop innovators are harnessing technological advancements to achieve financial liberation like never before. The times have changed, and the chains of old contracts have become irrelevant. A new generation is taking ownership on their own terms, paving the way for a brighter future.

CHAPTER 3

GOING FROM ARTIST TO ICON - WHEN BUSINESS GETS PERSONAL

When Jay-Z made the statement, "I'm overcharging for what they did to the Cold Crush, pay us like you owe us," he was demanding fair payment and recognition for the important contributions made by hip-hop pioneers like the Cold Crush Brothers. These pioneers often faced exploitation and financial injustices in the early days of the genre. Jay-Z wanted acknowledgment and fair treatment for their cultural impact.

As hip-hop grew in popularity and influence during the 2000s, elite performers transitioned from being just musicians to becoming iconic figures and influential celebrities. They built successful businesses and became ambassadors for brands across various industries, not just through their music but also through engaging in cultural conversations. Their albums sold in large volumes, turning them into corporate tycoons in their own right.

As hip-hop rose to prominence in the 2000s, iconic figures like Jay Z, Diddy, and Nelly became more than just talented artists. They became symbols of both artistic brilliance and entrepreneurial drive. But as they leveraged their coolness and lyrical talent to enter boardrooms and make business headlines, they also faced personal pressures and financial blunders.

Hip-hop reached unimaginable heights, with a market value of billions of dollars. However, beneath the surface, cracks in the industry's commercial foundation began to appear. These cracks exposed economic inequality and exploitation perpetuated by corporations, even affecting the most successful artists.

In this chapter, we take a close look at how hip-hop creators establish their personal brands, shape their lyrics, and live their lifestyles to create a strong bond with their fans. These artists skillfully seize business opportunities, transforming themselves into successful moguls. However, beneath the stories of going from humble beginnings to great success, there is a deeper narrative of financial struggles that reveals the complex nature of both the culture and business of hip-hop. It is crucial to acknowledge and understand these challenges in order to truly appreciate the growth and evolution of hip-hop.

In the early days, hip-hop artists saw the potential in turning their music into more than just songs. They understood that rap's commercial success required a different approach from traditional bands. Visionaries like Run DMC set the stage in the 80s by expanding their brand through collaborations with Adidas, while other iconic acts like the Fat Boys and Kurtis Blow landed major marketing deals with Burger King and Sprite. Hip-hop was more than just music, it was a platform for entrepreneurial success.

In the early days, commercial partnerships with urban artists were limited to one-off endorsement deals, lacking full integration into business structures. Cultural studies professor Tressie McMillan Cottom recognizes that these product relationships initially had narrow objectives, failing to see hip-hop's creators as versatile entrepreneurs; they were simply viewed as walking billboards promoting hip-hop beverages.

However, in the 21st century, hip-hop's biggest stars have become more than just musicians. They have evolved into successful entrepreneurs with a wide range of interests. From fashion and film to technology and various business ventures, these artists have taken on executive roles and built expansive portfolios. They are not just figureheads promoting other brands, but true artist-CEOs.

Research shows that the commercialization of hip-hop brands has been greatly influenced by the rise of digital media and technology. This has allowed hip-hop brands to expand their reach and capture the attention of mainstream audiences, coinciding with the increasing popularity of rap music in the mid-2000s.

One key factor in this expansion is the recognition by new artists and moguls of the opportunities presented by a wider demographic. In the past, hip-hop sponsorships primarily targeted young urban consumers. However, influential figures like Run-DMC paved the way for partnerships with brands like Adidas, which appealed to the niche urban apparel market. Today, artists such as Jay Z and Pharrell have strategically built reputations in high fashion and culture that reach beyond the traditional base of hip-hop, connecting with multiple social classes. This indicates a shift away from the racial assumptions that were once associated with the genre.

Similarly, they learned from past mistakes of undervaluing hip-hop's impact on the business world. Instead of simply capitalizing on its popularity, brands started to share the benefits with the creators. With the advent of Web 2.0, rap stars took control of their own stories and built sophisticated personal brands. This allowed them to not only create successful music careers, but also build profitable business portfolios and secure positions on corporate boards.

As Puff Daddy transformed into the marketing genius "Diddy" and climbed the ranks of the Highest Paid Entertainers, the hip-hop world began to prove its worth in the business world. Dr. Dre's massive deal with Beats headphones showed that hip-hop could sell technology while staying true to its roots. Now, lyrics are turning into profit, and hip-hop is taking control of the Wall Street scene. The tables have finally turned, and hip-hop is now running the show.

Hip-hop Icons turned their crafty nicknames into internationally recognized business brands demonstrating the fusion of hip-hop and entrepreneurship. This clever strategy has not only attracted urban youth, but also key demographics, extending the reach beyond just the music industry. The endorsement of Jay Z by former US President Barack Obama and the creative collaboration between Steve Jobs and Dr. Dre further solidify hip-hop's influence. These partnerships have ultimately led to substantial growth and success:

- Jay Z sells Rocawear for $204 million in 2007 and his Tidal music streamer to Square for $350 million in 2021 after Buying in at $56 million in 2015

- Diddy inks Ciroc vodka partnership earning over $100 million personal income by 2010

- Dr. Dre's Beats headphone line sells to Apple for $3 Billion in 2014 securing him position hip-hop's first ten-figure fortune

Influencer branding in hip-hop also took off in a big way during the 2010s. Nielsen discovered that over 75% of major advertisers were interested in partnering with hip-hop artists to boost their brands. Instead of just promoting products, these artists carefully chose which brands to align with based on their own personal style and image to become successful brand ambassadors in the hip-hop world.

In a game-changing move, hip-hop legends have transformed their personal brands into thriving empires. Instead of following fleeting trends or relying on temporary partnerships, these luminaries have strategically embedded their names and stories into every venture.

Unlike traditional celebrities who can be easily discarded or pushed aside once their usefulness for a campaign or product line ends, modern hip-hop hustlers have established themselves as powerful figures through self-ownership. Instead of simply licensing their image for a short period of time, these influencer CEOs have maintained control and strategically crafted their identity, creating enterprises that are deeply embedded with their names and stories.

Hip-Hop stars have become essential elements of popular culture, their stories infiltrating commercial platforms. Will Smith utilized his influence in Hollywood to become the first hip-hop actor turned producer, using Overbrook Entertainment as a means to finance and have creative control over his films. Diddy, on the other hand, not only mixed music and hosted Mix-tapes on radio shows but also established ownership of Revolt TV, a network that caters to urban music culture. Simultaneously, he leveraged his hustler businessman backstory to promote Ciroc Vodka and Sean John fashion. While ordinary celebrities may promote products temporarily, these hip-hop heavyweights personified brands that millennials have continually invested in for over a decade.

Iconic compilation albums like Jay Z's The Blueprint or 50 Cent's Get Rich or Die Trying strategically double as business manuals. Memorable lyrics like Biggie's "Spread love, it's the Brooklyn way" have transformed hip-hop hustling into thriving empires that continue to influence today. These albums trace the lineage of branding and serve as mission statements for success.

In the age of reality TV and social media, those on the forefront of hip-hop have become household names by combining artistic vision with commercial ambitions. These complex and flawed characters captivate audiences with their long-term character development. It's no longer enough to have one hit song and then be forgotten. These artists rely on their personas and personal endeavors to stay relevant in the hip-hop industry.

So, as brands were being established, hip-hop's entrepreneurs provided exclusive glimpses into their lives. They shared personal stories that kept audiences hooked, resulting in loyal fans who support Jay-Z's champagne or Nicki Minaj's Pink Friday lipstick, rather than just fleeting trends. Even supporting figures like Kanye West and Dame Dash always managed to capture attention with their bold statements and controversial business ventures.

As a result, hip-hop brands outshine traditional celebrity endorsements in growth and revenue, according to researchers at UT Austin. Over the course of several decades, leading hip-hop brands have seen nearly double the growth and annual revenues compared to their celebrity counterparts. In fact, while celebrity deals only manage to convert a single digit loyalty, hip-hop loyalists passionately support cultural architects, resulting in consistent conversion sales rates of 35-60%, as analyzed by the University of Arkansas.

Hip-hop has taken over the mainstream, making big moves in commerce. Artists are using their personas to secure deals and gain support from key demographics. They're showing their authentic origins and inspiring visions, winning over fans who become eager consumers. We're talking book deals from Russell Simmons and clothing lines from Nelly, Eve, Meek Mill, and more. It's not just about convenience – this is about building a loyal, intimate following.

In the past, brands used hip-hop struggles as marketing tools. But today's hip-hop artists have turned the tables, using big companies to promote community progress and black wealth. They're not just making money from music anymore – they're shaping culture and empowering their communities.

The rise of this innovative approach to showcasing the lives of hip-hop stars has brought both blessings and drawbacks. As soon as they made errors or fans discovered their favorites were not flawless, criticism became fair game. Hip-hop has created some of the most lucrative personal branding strategies in the business by combining entertainment and entrepreneurship, although not without enduring frequent tabloid scandals. Despite the downsides of intense scrutiny, hip-hop has quickly become a platform for transforming creative talent into commercial success, leading to the emergence of wealthy industry leaders ranked in Forbes every year.

Let's get one thing straight: just because there are plenty of opportunities doesn't mean all artists are rolling in money. Behind the flashy success stories of hip-hop, there's a hidden side full of challenges. It's not easy for artists to turn their lyrical talent into long-lasting wealth instead of fleeting fame. From failed brand deals to inconsistent income and even fraud, the financial game is tough for even the most successful hip-hop artists. They often have to shift their focus from their art to navigate the uncertain world of entrepreneurship.

In the fast-paced world of hip-hop, everyone seems to be starting their own businesses, from champagne brands to venture capital funds. But what about the flip side? What happens when these ambitious entrepreneurs fail to expand beyond music?

Turning fame into a profitable business is no small feat. Many businesses led by former chart-toppers have not only failed to generate consistent income, but have also tarnished their marketability due to lack of proper infrastructure. For instance, Ja Rule's credit card and clothing ventures famously failed, adding to his financial troubles and ultimately leading to his bankruptcy in the 2010s. In the era of the pandemic, artists like rapper Foogiano are exploring diverse avenues of income, including endorsing Trump-branded face masks, as a way to navigate hip-hop's challenging financial landscape.

Hip-Hop is more than just a passing trend, it's a vibrant culture. And if you want to succeed in this culture, you need to embrace it. Unfortunately, there are people out there who exploit this culture for their own gain. Recently, we've seen a surge in hip-hop reality shows trying to cash in on the success of Starz's hit show Power. These "culture vultures" are shamelessly trying to profit from the cultural capital of hip-hop without involving the actual creators and artists. For example, some construction executives from Utah tried to capitalize on a Power spinoff book series without the involvement of its creator, 50 Cent, by manipulating trademark claims. While a few shows like LeBron's Survivor's Remorse have managed to sustain interest in the hip-hop world, the majority end up fading away, chasing empty hype.

Also, don't underestimate the fact that businesses will always have their highs and lows. However, when you rely solely on hype to build your business, it becomes difficult for your supporters to stick with you during the tough times. The ones who make the most noise with their impressive success stories often hide even darker turmoil behind the scenes. It's as if they need to constantly put on a show to maintain their hip-hop business empires, despite the fact that it's just a matter of time before it all falls apart.

When Death Row Records was at its prime, it brought the party, chaos, and media frenzy like no other in the music industry. But even with all its success, corporate missteps led to bankruptcy and ultimately brought down Suge Knight, its notorious hip-hop founder. At one point we even seen Jay Z's TIDAL sale plummeting in value, temporarily watching his streaming service dreams take a hit. And that's not all - his liquor brand SC was facing legal battles over unpaid debts and losing its key players. It's a reminder that even the toughest brands can't escape some bruises.

And the examples just don't stop there... take Wu Tang's RZA, who faced a lawsuit from a co-founder of Wu Wear for allegedly selling shares he didn't fully own. And Lil Wayne fought for years with Cash Money heads over ambiguous contracts, denying him rightful ownership of his early recordings. The ups and downs of the business world can affect anyone, regardless of their fame.

Breaking away from the pack is crucial when building an influential business. Success is a science and requires a precise formula. Simply following the crowd won't cut it. Even in the rapidly expanding markets, many tequila brands raced to replicate Diddy's Ciroc success, but failed to come close to his ability to convert cultural influence into profitable nightlife ventures. Similarly, ambitious rap entrepreneurs flooded the cannabis industry, capitalizing on the initial legalization boom, but struggled to differentiate themselves from the hype and low margins of the big players.

Staying relevant in the business world requires staying on top of trends. But in the music industry, trends can be tricky. While some hip-hop icons successfully turn their influence into profitable ventures, the data shows that 75% of music business ventures face challenges. Many artists hope to establish sustainable franchises to support their creative endeavors, but often find themselves chasing fleeting trends. The idea of turning music into merchandise may seem lucrative, but financial realities have caused many hip-hop legends to crash and burn. Independence from labels may be the goal, but it's not always easy to achieve.

According to Professor Elodie D. Cable, research on the start-up scene shows that the average failure rate for entrepreneurs is around 60-80% in the best conditions. However, the hip-hop industry faces unique and systemic challenges that make the situation even more volatile. A study from the University of Delaware found that only 16% of rap entrepreneurs experience sustained growth after 5 years, while over 40% cease operations by the third year.

Despite hip-hop's long-standing admiration for ambitious hustlers who defy their circumstances, the reality check reveals that building sustainable companies in this industry can be extremely challenging, especially when compared to more established and supported fields. Trying to navigate the entertainment industry without a business background is already tough, but when you throw in the fact that mass incarceration disproportionately affects hip-hop artist and their network, the odds of achieving true success become even slimmer. The lack of a solid professional infrastructure further stacks the deck against aspiring entrepreneurs in this field.

Despite the challenges and data suggesting that it's difficult for hip-hop artists to turn influence and popularity into financial success, they still manage to defy the odds and avoid bankruptcy by taking a gamble on themselves. They continue to find ways to diversify their income and outperform the wider music industry, even as touring and streaming revenues decline.

University of Virginia arts research findings indicate that the 2010s saw a shift in the music industry, with many rappers starting their own side brands. These ventures are backed by a strong support system that includes financial services, mental health resources, and legal guidance. While the top tier of the hip-hop world may appear invincible, even they know that one bad business decision can jeopardize their success. This highlights the importance of staying alert and avoiding common pitfalls to keep the hip-hop industry financially stable.

So what about this generational wealth thing that we are constantly hearing about? How is it going for Hip-Hop Heirs and are they falling short?

One of the most heartbreaking aspects of hip-hop success stories is the struggle faced by the heirs left behind when the empire's architect passes away. While these architects enjoy a life of luxury and fame, their children often find themselves in a difficult position when the spotlight fades and they are left to carry on the legacy.

Headlines tell stories of former hip-hop royalty's downfall following the unexpected departure of their founders. Children of rap kings are left out of wills, iconic MC descendants air their family's dirty financial secrets in bitter estate disputes, and the empires built on temporary fame vanish overnight. This pattern repeats throughout hip-hop history, exposing the enormous challenge of converting temporary fame into lasting stability beyond the beats.

The NWA biopics have portrayed the rise to wealth of Dr. Dre and Ice Cube, emerging from their humble origins in Compton. However, what often goes unnoticed is the lack of financial literacy that has affected the daughter of their late peer, Easy E. Inheriting his Ruthless Records business, she struggles to navigate the complex world of finance without proper guidance. Despite the tremendous success and revenue generated by NWA's works long after Eazy's passing, he failed to leave a will or plan for the future, leaving his heirs vulnerable and potentially losing out on the spoils of his Hip-Hop dynasty that catalyzed the explosive rise of West Coast Rap. It's time we shed light on the importance of succession planning and protecting the interests of future generations in the ever-changing world of hip-hop.

Succession planning is crucial for safeguarding family legacies and preventing messy legal battles. Take the case of Lil Eazy E, the adopted son of the late rapper Eazy E. He fought against executives Jerry Heller and Bryan Turner, accusing them of wrongly collecting royalties and controlling Eazy E's music rights. This prevented the family from profiting from future earnings. Ultimately, widow Tomica Woods Wright sold her inheritance stake in Ruthless Records to Epic Records, completely separating the heirs from any future financial gains.

One person who stands out in this story is Erin Wright, the oldest daughter of Eazy E. She has struggled to get what she deserves from her father's will, along with her six siblings. Despite being part of Eazy E's music career as a child, Erin has faced homelessness and has openly criticized her family for leaving her in a desperate situation while they enjoy the wealth and fame. Her story reflects a common theme in hip-hop, where the transition from riches to rags is all too common.

Tupac Shakur's estate faced a hauntingly similar financial drama both after his death in the late-90s and his mother Afeni Shakur's passing 20 years later. Despite Tupac's undeniable impact on culture and his immense after death success with Death Row Records, the validity of the will was fiercely debated by his heirs after Afeni's recent death. While Tupac's music rights portfolio generated millions each year for 25 years through various channels, including music catalogs, clothing royalties, and Broadway adaptations of his lyrics, future generations struggled to reap the financial benefits and gain stability and ownership of their ancestor's hard-earned work.

Tupac's stepbrother, Mopreme Shakur, has come forward with a claim that their mom reneged on her promise to leave him inheritance gifts worth over $2 million in properties, which were verbally bequeathed by his iconic sibling. This ongoing battle sheds light on the challenges faced by heirs when it comes to managing assets and defending their rights. Meanwhile, filmmakers cash in on the revived popularity of Tupac with movies like All Eyez On Me, but face legal battles over the rights to portray his life on the big screen.

It's a sad reality that the immense musical legacies built by these iconic artists often slip through the fingers of their successors as soon as the memorial music fades. The untimely passings of rap legends like Biggie Smalls, Ol Dirty Bastard, Mac Dre, Proof (of D12 with Eminem), and many others have left behind complicated estate dilemmas, leaving their offspring without secure futures, despite the blockbuster catalogs these artists have left behind.

The staggering amounts of money generated after their deaths highlight the painful reality for the close-knit circles surrounding beloved hip-hop legends. These late icons' inheritances are slowly depleted as their children are left unaware of the lucrative business deals. A recent lawsuit exposed

Elvis Presley's estate totaling over $1 billion solely from his music assets. Michael Jackson's estate came close to half a billion dollars before his heirs took charge. Even lesser-known blues artist James Peterson Radio received a surprising windfall of $37 million from royalties of a riff he wrote 60 years ago, which was featured in a popular iPhone commercial.

Why do heirs of hip-hop icons, who have earned billions in the modern era of cultural media, often face destitution, blackballing, and a loss of identity when their patriarchs tragically pass away too soon? It's clear as day: Greed, a lack of long-term planning, and unfair systems are stopping wealth from being passed on to the next generations. Families are fighting over the direction of businesses and rushing to cash in on media rights, tours, merchandise, and even buying up entire labels after the deaths of hip-hop legends.

They say if you keep doing the same thing, you'll get the same results. It's time to make a change. Instead of fixing the old, let's focus on building something new. Rather than using our existing resources to guarantee future success, we need to invest in the next generation and create opportunities for them. According to researchers at the University of Houston, we need to take a long-term view and prioritize building wealth through hip-hop culture. It's time to think differently and ensure a prosperous future for the hip-hop community.

Don't let our legends' legacy go to waste! The lack of support for up-and-coming talent leaves the next generation of hip-hop artists in a vulnerable position, with no guidance or knowledge of the resources available to them. We need to ensure that the creative autonomy of these artists is protected and celebrated. Let's not just briefly mourn our fallen icons before moving on to the next big thing - let's honor them by supporting the new wave of talent and pushing for a sustainable and authentic music industry.

Hip-hop moguls of the past paved the way for the next generation, overcoming obstacles and breaking societal norms. These gamechangers, like Jay Z, Dr. Dre, and Diddy, achieved extraordinary success despite unconventional backgrounds. However, their heirs still face unpredictable challenges due to existing disparities. This is particularly true for female artists in hip-hop, who usually struggle to provide for their children while pursuing their artistic passions. The high cost of education often stifles their creative potential.

Again, hip-hop, a booming industry worth billions, still grapples with long-standing disparities especially when it comes to women in the genre. These inequities pose significant challenges for female artists, producers, and entrepreneurs navigating the hip-hop ecosystem and more importantly for Hip-Hop as a whole.

As Martin Luther King Jr. profoundly stated, "Injustice anywhere is a threat to justice everywhere." This timeless wisdom holds true not only in the broader context of civil rights but also within the realm of hip-hop. When we fail to treat women in hip-hop fairly, we perpetuate an injustice that reverberates throughout the entire industry. These women, who often play pivotal roles in raising the next generation of hip-hop artists, are the bedrock upon which the genre's future is built. Empowering them, ensuring they receive equitable compensation and opportunities, is not only a matter of moral imperative but also a means to sustain financial freedom for the heirs of hip-hop. By acknowledging and rectifying the disparities faced by women in hip-hop, we pave the way for families to enjoy the fruits of their ancestors' hard work and create a legacy of generational wealth based on a foundation of justice and equality.

These disparities include but not limited to:

Pay Gap: Despite reaching similar levels of success, female hip-hop artists consistently earn less than their male counterparts. This financial imbalance pervades record sales, streaming royalties, and even concert earnings. It's time we bridge this gap and ensure fair compensation.

Breaking the Glass Ceiling: Women remain underrepresented in executive and decision-making roles, translating to unequal opportunities for female artists and entrepreneurs. It's time to level the playing field and provide equal chances for success.

Empowerment and Ownership: Female artists deserve full control and ownership of their work, including songwriting rights, master recordings, and creative direction. Let's empower them to reap the benefits of their hard work and talent.

Access to Resources: Limited access to financial backing, studio time, and marketing budgets creates barriers for female artists. By providing equitable access to resources, we can amplify their voices and help them thrive in a competitive industry.

Shattering Stereotypes: Gender-based stereotypes and misogyny hold female artists back from expressing their creativity and securing collaboration and sponsorship opportunities. It's time to challenge these stereotypes and create an inclusive environment where everyone can flourish.

Intersectional Challenges: Women of color face unique obstacles in hip-hop, compounding income disparities and affecting career longevity. Let's address these intersectional challenges head-on to ensure equality for all.

Recognizing these challenges, it's crucial to prioritize diversity, equity, and inclusion in hip-hop. Female artists, in particular, have long struggled with disparities in pay, representation, ownership, and access to resources. To ensure a prosperous future for hip-hop, industry-wide initiatives must bridge these gaps, offering fair compensation, equal opportunities, and a supportive environment for women in hip-hop.

Despite these hurdles, female artists in hip-hop continue to defy expectations and achieve remarkable success. The likes of Missy Elliott, Nicki Minaj, and Cardi B have shattered glass ceilings, proving women's immense talent and market potential in the genre.

As we navigate the ever-changing landscape of hip-hop, we must not forget the struggles faced by the heirs of iconic artists. Succession planning and financial literacy are essential to secure the legacy and financial stability of future generations. By addressing these issues and empowering women in hip-hop, we honor the past, support the present, and create a more equitable and prosperous future for the entire hip-hop community.

PART II: EMPOWERMENT

CHAPTER 4

FOLLOWING THE MONEY - UNDERSTANDING HIP-HOP ECONOMICS

Hip-hop's rise from underground movement to multi-billion dollar industry is an economic story as much as a cultural one. To fully understand hip-hop's potential for empowerment, we need to follow the money trail and analyze the financial machinery powering its commercial success.

In this chapter, we'll study the anatomy of hip-hop economics - investigating the major money-making machines, revenue streams, and artist income models across the decades. These systems have fueled hip-hop's growth for 50 years, but transparency around the data has been murky at best. By confronting the financial truths head-on, we can start rewriting hip-hop's business practices to be more empowering for its creators.

Let's jump straight into the numbers:

Hip-Hop/R&B surpassed rock in 2017 as the dominant music genre in the U.S. for the first time in history. It now accounts for ~30% of total music industry revenues, topping pop and rock.

The global hip-hop market has ballooned into a $30 billion dollar industry as of 2022 - spanning recorded music, fashion, endorsements, touring, and corporate partnerships.

Music/entertainment market research group MRC Data shows annual hip-hop revenues growing at faster clip than the overall music industry.

So how have these astronomical numbers been generated and where is the money actually going?

Following The Streams: Unpacking Hip-Hop's Digital Revenue Revolution

In the early 2000s, hip-hop artists were on shaky ground. Album sales were plummeting, digital piracy was rampant, and their label agreements were falling apart. However, in the last decade, streaming has come to the rescue, revolutionizing how music is distributed and providing valuable data-driven financial management.

Hip-hop is now both the most consumed and fastest growing genre in music streaming. According to Spotify, in 2020 rap received over 28% of total global streams.

While radio and MTV were once vital for exposure, playlist programming and serving personalized hip-hop content to engaged fans is now driving the discoverability and revenues.

In this section, we explore how streaming and digital mediums are fueling the financial growth of hip-hop, revitalizing its economy.

Tracking The Streams: Hip-Hop Streaming Dominance

MRC Group's music industry analytics demonstrate hip-hop's dominance on DSPs (digital service providers like Spotify and Apple Music):

- Hip-hop accounted for over 30% of streams in 2021 - its largest share yet

- Rap catalog streaming annually grows 19.9% outpacing all other genres

- Flagship hip-hop playlists like RapCaviar drive significant share of platform consumption

As consumption patterns rapidly shift, streaming now accounts for over 75% of US hip-hop recorded revenue - more than triple physical format sales.

Decoding Artist Streaming Income

But how much are artists actually earning from streams? Since hip-hop pulls in the largest streaming share, its imperative to understand the rev share model.

Though calculations vary by distributor and label deal, here is approximate streaming payout breakdown:

- Per stream artist royalty range: $0.003-0.005

- To earn monthly minimum wage of $1580 with a 0.004 payout = 395,000 streams

According to a top digital distribution exec " unless you have serious scale, streaming checks don't amount to much money for the average rap artist."

A mid-tier hip-hop act needs to pull over 20 million yearly streams to gross just around $100K annually from Spotify alone. That requires a fanbase of 200-300k monthly listeners to maintain - a very high bar for most. For context - getting 1 million monthly Spotify listeners enters Top 200 most followed territory.

However, for rap superstars streaming income is a cash cow. Since hip-hop dominates consumption, it means bigger royalty checks for its stars.

Drake topped Artists of the Decade with over 28 billion streams. Experts estimate his streaming royalties nearing 9 figures per year just from his back catalog. Rap star Post Malone recently crossed a staggering 10 billion streams at the time of this writing.

As scale increases, streaming payout compound for successful hip-hop artists in a way unmatched historically. Catalog depth pays - enabling creative freedom.

Turning Viral Smashes Into Cash Flow

Of course hip-hop artists still pursue mainstream hits to capture cultural moments, spike streams, and generate cash flow.

While viral hip-hop tracks present marketing opportunities, converting momentum into [$] requires unlock reads, pre-saves, quality followings and proven business infrastructure.

Case Study: Arizona Zervas

Arizona Zervas' 2019 viral hit "Roxanne" off indie label 10K Projects peaked at over 40 million streams/month on Spotify alone during its hype cycle - an incredible independent breakout.

However, despite the song's TikTok explosion, Zervas had to quickly strategize beyond the meme hype and prove his artistic depth and touring ability to build a sustainable career as a young hip-hop act. He's now signed to Columbia Records and working towards his debut studio album.

Forget about the viral splash and fleeting hype. If a lasting income is what artists are after, it's all about consistent quality content, building a strong bond with fans, and harnessing the power of touring.

Labels and artists alike reap long-term rewards when they play the "career game" instead of mindlessly chasing after every social media trend.

In this ever-changing landscape, it's time to focus on what truly matters. Let's dive into the strategies that will transform artistic journey into a sustainable source of income.

Diversifying Digital: YouTube, Gaming & Social Cash

To supplement streaming income, hip-hop artists also monetize massive audiences on YouTube and gaming channels with advert share and paid digital experiences.

Hip-hop again crushes other genres for YouTube video views - accounting for over 30% of content. Unsigned artists also leverage the platform to globally distribute music and premium video content from their channels.

However, controversial changes to advertiser guidelines called Adpocalypse limited monetization of hip-hop artists in recent years due to lyrical content. Alternatives like Patreon allow creators more autonomy.

Hip-hop artists have also dominated music gaming integration- partnering with Fortnite for virtual concerts and having their songs included on networks like Twitch for subscriptions and live streams.

And direct-to-consumer offerings provide premium perks for top fans from Discord channels to member-only merch.

Case Study: Soulja Boy

Soulja Boy remains a pioneer of hip-hop's digital hustle - amassing over 15 million YouTube subscribers and billions of historical streams.

As royalties slowed and his comeback album faced delays, Soulja in 2018 pivoted efforts towards gaming - attracting nearly 3 million followers on Twitch through Fortnite, Call of Duty and more.

Between gaming profits, real estate holdings and independent music he reportedly earns $30 million annually - largely thanks to digitally direct fan engagement.

So Who Are The Key Players In Hip-Hop's Financial Food Chain?

In the 2000's - companies like Interscope, Roc-A-Fella, No Limit and Cash Money built empires almost entirely on hip-hop's growing commercial appeal. 50 Cent's Get Rich Or Die Trying remains one of the most financially successful rap albums ever for a label.

But over the past decade - consolidation of major labels and diversified streaming platforms has drastically changed the landscape.

Let's analyze some of the modern Industry players powering hip-hop's financial revolution:

Universal Music Group (UMG)

The world's largest music company, UMG captured over a third of 2020 global industry revenues.

Through labels like Republic, Aftermath and Def Jam plus distribution channel Island Records, UMG has an all-star hip-hop roster: Drake, Lil Wayne, Eminem, Rihanna, J.Cole, Nicki, Future, Nas, Kanye, Kendrick + many more.

Acquiring artists' catalog rights (ex. Taylor Swift, Bob Dylan) also gives UMG a longer-term lock on asset appreciation as streaming revenues continues to grow into the future.

Hip-hop, R&B and Pop accounted for roughly 80% of UMG's 2021 recorded revenues proving the genres commercial dominance and importance to its growth.

UMG often draws critiques of consolidating too much artist and label equity - potentially limiting future independence. But chairman Lucian Grainge calls protecting the creative community "even more important than economics."

Sony Music Group

Key Labels: RCA Records, Columbia Records + Partnerships - "THE ORCHARD"

Rosters: Doja Cat, Lil Nas X, Tyler The Creator, ASAP Rocky, DJ Khaled + other global stars

Strategy: Acquire emerging rap talent and support artistic development

Sony has taken a venture capital approach- investing early in young hip-hop artists like Lil Tecca then providing resources and runway for them to mature into superstars like Doja hitting #1 debuts.

Warner Music Group (WMG)

Atlantic Records: Leads Warner charge in hip-hop w/ Cardi B, Jack Harlow, Lil Uzi Vert, Wiz Khalifa, Gucci Mane, Saweetie

300 Entertainment: Key Strategic JV Partnership w/ Young Thug's label (signed Megan Thee Stallion helping break female rapper glass ceilings)

Independent Leverage: Warner acquired artists rights companies like IMGN, EMPEMLA and assets like David Guetta recordings showing ability to diversify.

WMG's independent distribution network has helped market hip-hop acts like Gunna, Lil Durk, NLE Choppa, Polo G, and EST Gee giving them resources to grow loyal fan bases. Access to radio promotion teams and digital marketing strategists proved vital for these artists getting early career momentum.

By allowing artists to maintain ownership of masters and leverage label expertise/relationships, Warner forges strong partnerships in hip-hop's competitive space. Meek Mill signing a JV label deal with WMG in 2022 shows a symbolic shift as he has been outspoken on past label disputes and advocate for artist rights.

Spotify

As the global streaming leader, Spotify is built off hip-hop's mainstream appeal.

Flagship hip-hop playlists like RapCaviar command almost 13 million followers. Spotify knows hip-hop's importance - recently launching its first dedicated major hub "Clash" to highlight new rap talent and uniquely showcase catalogs.

Controversies around lack of artist data transparency, threats to pull music, and royalty debates have somewhat soured artist relations however.

Spotify has tested non-fungible tokens (NFTs) and announced plans to expand livestream concerts/events natively - exploring new ways to keep hip-hop artists monetizing engagement on their platform directly.

YouTube

YouTube has become the world's most popular on-demand music streaming app with over 2 billion monthly music listeners.

Hip-hop represented a staggering 30% share of YouTube music content in 2021. From emerging artists distributing songs to superstars like Drake premiering albums and building video content channels - it's a vital part of marketing campaigns now.

However, "Adpocalypse" advertiser rule changes and cracking down on sample/copyright claims created obstacles for hip-hop artists using the platform freely and impaired monetization for some. However, the platform remains crucial for these artists despite these obstacles.

TikTok

TikTok has risen as a breakout force for hip-hop discovery and consumption amongst Gen Z.

Beyond viral dance/song trends, hip-hop artists use TikTok to steer cultural narrative and conversation while previewing new music.

Rolling Stone called TikTok "new early warning system" for hip-hop hits as data shows it's becoming a leading indicator for streaming trajectory on Spotify/Apple.

Triller

Triller positions itself as a competitor app to TikTok with focus on hip-hop - raw, authentic, creative expression. Triller has become known as the destination for hip-hop artists to debut new tracks, album trailers, behind the scenes content.

Triller's monthly active user base has surged threefold from 2020 to 2021, fueled by explosive Verzuz battles, captivating Jake Paul fight streaming deals, and dynamic partnerships centered around original hip-hop content.

With Triller, artists become stakeholders and receive equity in the company via song partnership deals. Swizz Beatz, Eminem, Alicia Keys are all involved. Triller gives artists more ownership and control.

Snapchat

Snapchat proves hip-hop resonance amongst coveted young users - 40% of Gen Z log into the app daily.

From AR filters to premium Shows, Snap provides monetization and amplification touchpoints for hip-hop artists' digital marketing strategies.

Travis Scott's virtual Fortnite concert success actually began as an augmented reality performance in Snapchat in 2019.

Hip-hop artists recognize Snaps power to drive conversion + build early momentum for releases.

Web3 & Blockchain Platforms

Hip-hop collectors, influencers and artists flock to Web3 platforms like Doodles, Yuga Labs and Polygon seeking ownership. They deliver new models for digital goods/items supporting creator economies.

Cryptocurrencies allow direct exchange of value between artist/fan while avoiding middlemen. NFTs verify exclusive/limited access passes, art and music content representing next wave for artist revenue.

We'll explore blockchain disruption more later but its opening new creative doors for hip-hop and shifting power back from corporations to the people.

Now Breaking It Down: Modern Rapper Economics - Where Does The Cash Come From?

In Web 2.0 - as major label ties loosened and 360 deals declined, independence became more possible for hip-hop artists to build careers leveraging streaming and multimedia.

Revolutionary hip-hop acts like Nipsey Hussle and Chance The Rapper showed artists could compete, selling almost 100,000+ units without labels.

While rap superstars like Drake, Nicki Minaj, and Cardi B enjoy immense wealth from various sources such as touring, sponsorships, investments, and royalties, we need to also examine how breakthrough mid-tier and rising artists eat in the game today.

Striking The Streaming Lottery

It's no secret that hip-hop has the most lucrative record royalties given its streaming leadership position. Just look at the top 25 most streamed artists ever - hip-hop dominates nearly every slot.

When an artist catches fire on DSPs - the consistent passive income takes their career to new heights and offers creative freedom.

Let's look at breakthrough Virginia rapper Roddy Ricch:

After the Billboard #1 smash "The Box" exploded as the highest charting hip-hop debut single since 1992 and streamed over 2 billion times in 2 years - Roddy has since invested streaming success into diverse income sources:

- Signed lucrative deal with Atlantic Records for $15M+

- Launched rare sneaker NFT collab fetching $55k bids

- Booking $150k+ nightly fees for 40-city tour in 2022

So while Roddy's music makes impressive bank from streams/sales, the leverage and credibility factor accelerates additional business ventures.

Cashing In On Concert Mania

Live performances have become more important than ever with decline of recorded music profits. Top rappers push 8 figures grossing huge global arena and festival tours.

Let's use rap chart-topper Polo G as a case study:

Polo G catapulted to stardom off Columbia Records in 2019. By his junior album in 2022 he's commanding $70k-$100k nightly for his 85-stop Hall of Fame World Tour grossing over $10 million.

And that's not all:

- Pulling 7 figures annually from drink company Body Armour sponsorship deal

- Retailing successful Nike/Polo G merch collab sneaker

- Interacting 1-on-1 with superfans via Cameo side hustle raking in over $1k per personalized clip

Again, this illustrates how one successful artist parallels into outside business flows.

As The New York Times recently analyzed "2021 became the Year of the Rap Tour" - outpacing pop acts. Hip-hop tours accounted for 19 of the top 35 grossing treks as rap connoisseurs yearn for live shows.

And make no mistake - these rappers eat off shows. Polo G's tour will gross him more cash than he likely made off his top 10 Fame album in 2022. Especially given 360 deal pressures.

Monetizing Digital Real Estate

While previously discussed, artists also leverage Their massive Instagram, YouTube, TikTok channels for both engagement and income.

Back to Roddy... although quieter recently, he has 14.5 million IG followers and 1 billion TikTok video views in the past years where he pushes content/music sneak peaks.

Controlling and properly commercializing this digital territory is vital. YouTube ads, merch links, NFT integrations offer monetization paths tied to the audience.

And hip-hop artists with big followings like Roddy charge $100k+ for a branded IG post or club cameo because of its direct marketing value. Gotta maximize your network!

Bringing Web3 Flavor

Rappers also pioneer digital innovation - promoting NFT collections, launching tokens and staking claims in blockchain ecosystems hoping to bring ownership back to artists.

It not only unlocks new profit channels but also reinforces their influencer credibility and disrupter aura for being ahead of trends.

We'll dig deeper into Web3 disruption later but its opening creative funding/direct monetization doors. Over $4 billion was spent on NFTs in one calendar year alone.

In order to maintain cultural relevance and avoid financial exploitation like they did in the past, hip-hop artists must keep pushing boundaries into new digital territory. It is crucial for them to break free from any constraints and navigate through the politics of the music industry. By doing so, they can sustain their influence and impact in today's ever-changing landscape.

The Path to Financial Freedom: Navigating Labels, Distribution + Ownership Rights

In today's day and age hip-hop artists have more options than ever before to professionally record and distribute music to build their careers. Let's explore different avenues, from label partnerships to independent self-releasing projects, that empower artists to take control of their own destiny.

Major Label System

The major label pipeline (UMG, Sony, Warner) still develops superstars leveraging bags, marketing dollars and boots on the ground.

In exchange for funding recording/videos and providing upfront artist payments they generally control rights and secure revenue shares for 3–7-year periods. Intense competition has moved deals toward 50/50 net profit splits vs past 80/20 arrangements but still requires big breaks to generate artist income.

Artists McDaniel calls label services "long money" with patience and release commitment being key. Data shows less than 5% ever fully pay back advances through sales.

Major labels incentivize artists to stay "inside their system" by analyzing data to identify commercially successful performers. While this tried-and-true model offers stability, it also requires artists to conform to certain expectations.

Venture Partnership Deals

For hip-hop artists with some momentum, small VC-backed studios like 10K Projects, Alamo, LVRN, Victor Records emerge as label alternatives. They spot talent earlier, co-create rather than dictate artistic vision and incentivize longer term success over quick hits. They maintain a partnership mentality.

Examples like WWE Superstar John Cena and the Boston venture fund behind 10K Projects demonstrate the ability to spot viral hits like Arizona Zervas' "Roxanne" in 2019 and guiding his development. These industry experts strike a balance between artist creative freedom and growth marketing expertise, ensuring successful outcomes.

Independent & Self-Release

Today's digital tools also allow hip-hop artists independence at earlier stages. Avoiding label politics or rinse-repeat song cycles.

Chance The Rapper famously tapped into streaming and social media for his Grammy winning Coloring Book album rollout - a pioneering inde artist case study. He also self-released his latest album, maneuvering around the major label route.

Rappers jack Harlow and Russ grew initial fanbases off catchy self-released projects - strategically feeding consistent content to Spotify playlists before signing major label deals from positions of leverage.

Distributors like EmuBands, DistroKid, and CD Baby provide a game-changing opportunity for artists. With direct artist uploads and access to premium playlist channels, these platforms empower artists to take control of their music careers like never before.

Others like Frank Ocean, Westside Gunn built their own companies. While independence means more responsibility, self-made hip-hop acts retain rights ownership.

Web3 Decentralization

Blockchain models are revolutionizing the way artists connect with supporters and raise funds for their creative projects. Through peer-to-peer exchanges of value, artists can directly engage with their audience while securing new income streams. This groundbreaking technology empowers hip-hop artists to take control of their digital goods ownership, unlocking endless possibilities for financial growth and creative expression.

For example below are some Web3 projects that Hip-Hop artist are taking advantage of:

- Hip-hop NFT art/collectibles (Fetty Wap, Nas, Future)

- Pre-sale token access passes (Soulja Boy, Lil Yachty)

- Virtual performances in digital spaces like The Wave powered by Solana

- Song sales/distributions via platforms like Opulous

Web3 puts opportunity directly into hip-hop artists hands vs labels while reshaping fan participation into creator economies.

The Rise of the Raptrepreneur Business Model

Hip-hop's explosive success has given rise to a new breed of entrepreneurial pioneers, known as the "rappreneur class." These savvy hustlers are not content with just making music; they are launching their own companies and forging futures beyond the confines of the industry.

Radio Hall of Famer and television personality Lenard McKelvey aka Charlamagne tha God details hip-hop's growing "boss infrastructure and generational wealth opportunity".

Since corporations historically denied fair access and growth in America, McKelvey praises how hip-hop continues to " skillfully build its own thriving ecosystem and overcome systemic obstacles."

We'll spotlight rapper entrepreneurial ventures later, but today's social/digital media combined with the hip-hop hustler spirit makes success more tangible.

Rappers Getting Active

From Jay Z's champagne to Dr Dre's headphones, rapper branded business success stories have inspired modern artists to also push entrepreneurial pursuits.

Everyone wants to rap today but also push their own brands. With the rise of social media, we now have unprecedented opportunities for direct-to-consumer connection and sales conversion. It's a game-changer like never before.

Today we see rappers getting busy:

- Pusha T - Arby's Campaigns

- Nelly - Applebees Partnerships

- Travis Scott - PlayStation Creative Director

- 2 Chainz Kesha Vodka/Restaurants

- Cardi B Fashionnova Clothing Collab $$

- G Herbo & Hitmaka Real Estate Plays

- Nas & Lil Yachty Crypto Exchange Ventures

The rap hustle mentality has fueled these artist-entrepreneurs to identify untapped opportunities and utilize their influence to secure lucrative ventures beyond music.

Inspired by the Spiritual Rebel Model

Hip-hop has long embraced a spirit of rebellious entrepreneurship, with artists creating ventures that not only address cultural needs but also give back to their communities.

Nipsey Hussle followed this model until his tragic 2019 passing. He independently sold $100 mixtapes, purchased local real estate to revitalize his Crenshaw neighborhood, built The Marathon Store as a community hub, invested in restaurant partnerships, which all brought in ownership opportunities for him, his family and community.

In death, his legacy soared even higher. A reserved parking spot NFT at Marathon store sold for an astonishing $250k at AGUIX. But that's not all. His life rights were also acquired by Amazon Studios for a whopping $15M.

Nipsey rejected major label deals - maintaining full control over his content/vision. He channeled his passion into assets and not liabilities. The Nipsey model lives on through artist like LaRussell; Like Nipsey, who rejected major label deals to maintain control over his content, LaRussell is pioneering change in hip hop by building an independent brand based on authenticity and ethics. Through his collective "Good Compenny," LaRussell provides resources for artists to execute their ideas without giving up ownership. His movement allows people to pay what they want, making his contributions priceless. With vivid storytelling ability comparable to rap greats, LaRussell creates relatable art. After his 2021 freestyle went viral, the world took notice. With co-signs from influencers like Charlamagne da God and Meek Mill, LaRussell and his brand follow Nipsey's model of ownership and community upliftment.

Hip-Hop As Venture Capital

Hip-hop moguls are now becoming venture capital powerhouses themselves. They are not just dominating the music industry, but also investing in and advising startups, expanding their entrepreneurial reach like never before. These influential figures are using their expertise and resources to support new ventures and make a significant impact in the business world.

Take JAY-Z, who founded Marcy Venture Partners. This venture capital firm focuses on funding minority founders and women-led startups. Notable investments include Rihanna's Savage X Fenty and securing early equity in the successful sports trading company, Dapper Labs.

Another example is Dr. Dre, who strategically positioned Aftermath Entertainment to discover talented artists and produce captivating content. One of their notable successes is 50 Cent's Branson Cognac and the production of TV series.

In today's landscape, we have seen a rise in black-owned venture firms, with over 109 currently in existence. For instance, Concrete Rose Capital is making significant investments in digital healthcare and education, signaling the expansion of hip-hop hustler talent into more sophisticated industries.

Here's a list additional Venture Capital Firms with Hip-Hop Adjacent Investors

1. **A16z Cultural Leadership Fund (CLF):** is Silicon Valley's first venture capital fund consisting of 100% African American Limited Partners cofounded by Chris Lyons who started his career in the music industry working for Grammy-Award-winning producer Jermaine Dupri. Some of A16z CLF Investors include Pharrell William, Anderson Paak, The Weeknd, Earn Your Leisure, among others.

2. **Queensbridge Venture Partners:** Founded by Nasir "Nas" Jones and Anthony Saleh, this venture capital firm focuses on early-stage technology companies. Through QVP, Nas has an impressive investment portfolio, backing companies with significant valuations. Just take a look at some of his investments: Dropbox with a valuation of $10 billion, Lyft valued at $5.5 billion, Tilt with a valuation of $400 million, and Robinhood, which raised an impressive $50 million in Series B funding.

3. **Upfront Ventures:** Upfront Ventures is a venture capital firm based in Los Angeles, California. Formerly known as GRP Partners, it was founded in 1996 and rebranded as Upfront Ventures in 2013. Chamillionaire (Hakeem Seriki), is a Limited Partner who joined as an entrepreneur-in-residence in 2015. Chamillionaire brings a wealth of experience from his involvement in various

investments and business ventures. As the founder of Chamillitary Entertainment, he has proven himself not only in the music industry but also as a savvy entrepreneur.

4. **Casa Verde Capital:** Casa Verde Capital is a venture capital firm that focuses on investments in the cannabis industry. It was founded in 2015 by Calvin Broadus Jr., better known as Snoop Dogg, along with Karan Wadhera and Ted Chung.

5. **Mag Ventures, Acorn Ventures:** Acorn Ventures is a venture capital firm that invests in early-stage technology companies. Russell Simmons, the visionary behind Def Jam Records and multiple successful clothing lines, is an investor in this venture. Teaming up with Acorn Ventures and MAG Ventures, he invested $5 million in Flyp, a groundbreaking company that revolutionizes how we use phone numbers. Flyp allows you to have multiple phone numbers on a single device, giving you the flexibility to separate work and personal calls effortlessly. This innovative solution empowers individuals to take control of their communication needs.

6. **S30 Inc:** SC30 Inc. is the business entity established by Steph Curry, the greatest 3-point shooter on the planet and in NBA's history. SC30 Inc. serves as his personal brand and investment vehicle. Some notable investments by SC30 Inc. include companies like Palm, Slyce, and SnapTravel.

7. **Vista Equity Partners:** is a private equity firm that specializes in investing in software, data, and technology-enabled companies. Founded by Robert F Smith, Billionaire and the richest black man in American History

These examples highlight the immense impact that individuals from diverse backgrounds are making in the world of business. It is a testament to their resilience and entrepreneurial spirit.

Bringing It All Together: Case Study - Drake's Financial Formula

No current rapper has built their brand or maximized their clout better commercially than Drake. He remains the blueprint for transforming rap stardom into a diverse generational wealth portfolio.

Let's analyze the empire Drake is architecting - powered by streaming royalty riches but also smart diversification:

Stable Record Income

Drake, the music industry's "big streaming winner," earns an astounding 25-150 million dollars in annual royalty checks from his recordings, making him rap's richest current earner according to Forbes. This massive income not only fuels his success in the music world but also attracts companies who eagerly seek access and insight into his audience.

The Undisputed Tour/Show Powerhouse

According to an eye-opening Billboard feature published on November 2, 2023, the undisputed king of hip-hop is none other than Drake himself. Claiming the coveted top spot on the list of Top 20 Grossing Hip-Hop Acts of All Time, Drake raked in a mind-boggling $472.9 million with over 300 electrifying tour shows under his belt. His shows are can't-miss bucket list experiences that leave even the biggest pop stars in his dust.

Digital Leader Brand

Selling almost 130 million records and boasting over 100 million Instagram followers, Drake has truly become a master of leveraging digital channels and marketing to amplify his events. From showcasing album art on iconic Toronto landmarks to implementing creative social media strategies, he serves as an inspiring case study for direct-to-consumer conversion in the modern era.

Culture Connector Ventures

Leveraging his cultural influence and business acumen, Drake is using his company DreamCrew to build an empire through strategic investments and partnerships. With co-founder Adel "Future" Nur, DreamCrew serves as a platform for Drake to pursue his diverse interests. As executive producer, Drake has used the company's production arm to deliver hit shows like Euphoria and Top Boy on HBO and Netflix. By aligning with elite talents like LeBron James, Drake and DreamCrew continue to expand their entertainment and business network. With Drake's brand power opening doors, DreamCrew allows him to turn his varied ambitions into lucrative business realities.

Passionfruit Portfolio

Unlocking new income channels and investing in key cultural growth markets, Drake is diversifying his holdings across alcohol, cannabis, gaming, and real estate assets. With an estimated 8-figure stake in the rapidly growing Cashmere cannabis industry, he's seizing opportunities and capitalizing on emerging trends. Some of his key investments and partnerships include:

- Sports media company Overtime - Drake joined other high-profile investors like Jeff Bezos to invest $80 million into this company that creates sports content for social media platforms.
- Plant-based food company Daring Foods - Drake participated in a $40 million funding round for this maker of plant-based chicken

products. The market for faux chicken is seen as having major growth potential.
- Online investment platform Wealthsimple - Drake was part of a massive $750 million funding round for this Canadian fintech startup now valued at over $5 billion.
- Restaurant chain Dave's Hot Chicken - Drake invested an undisclosed sum into this quick-service restaurant focusing on hot chicken that is aggressively expanding locations across North America.

So in summary, Drake is placing strategic bets across sports media, food, fintech and restaurants - indicating his business interests are diversified. His recent pace of deals signals he is ramping up investments to grow his portfolio.

Back To The 6ix Impact

Drake, like Jay Z with Marcy Venture Partners, is making a significant impact on the city of Toronto. Through DreamCrew, he not only promotes Canadian artists and founders but also supports infrastructure projects in his hometown. His dedication to elevating "The 6" and putting Canada on the global stage is commendable.

In a recent collaboration with the iconic CN Tower, Drake brought joy to children and instilled a sense of national pride. This intricate partnership showcased his commitment to the city and the entire country.

According to marketing and branding consultant Gordon Hendren, Drake's influence is responsible for about 5 percent of Toronto's annual tourism income, totaling $8.8 billion. The hip-hop icon's ability to attract visitors showcases his significant impact on the city's economy.

Beyond his musical career, Drake has proven himself as an entrepreneur by founding the OVO Sound record label in 2012 with longtime collaborator 40. In 2013, he was appointed as the "global ambassador" for the Toronto Raptors basketball team, joining its executive committee.

Drake's passion for his city and dedication to promoting Canadian talent make him a true influencer both locally and internationally.

The Road Ahead: Rewriting The Rules of Hip-Hop Economics

Hopefully, this analysis has revealed the inner workings of hip-hop's financial landscape. We delved into the billions in revenues, streaming payouts, label dynamics, and other factors that shape rapper income. We uncovered the truth behind the financial machinery of hip-hop and gained a deeper understanding of this fascinating industry.

The future looks bright and promising as hip-hop's mainstream popularity continues to skyrocket, leaving stale rock and pop formats in the dust. This exciting growth projection gives us every reason to be optimistic about what lies ahead.

However we know past unfair deals have hindered too many artists from properly eating fruits of their labor and building wealth.

Pioneers like Nipsey Hussle and Drake have demonstrated the importance of maintaining ownership, creative freedom, and access to unbiased financial resources. Their pioneering efforts highlight the need for hip-hop artists to take control of their careers and navigate the industry with a fierce determination. By owning their work, maintaining artistic integrity, and securing reliable financial support, these artists have paved the way for others to follow suit. It's time for aspiring rappers to seize these opportunities and forge their own path towards long-lasting success in the music industry.

The road ahead must prioritize:

1) **Education/Mentorship** - arming artists with business/financial knowledge

2) **Policy Reform** - advocating for equitable streaming royalty models

3) **Venture Investment** - funding diverse hip-hop entrepreneurial pursuits

4) **Technological Innovation** - boosting blockchain models supporting independence

Hip-hop's billion-dollar economy is on the rise, and it's crucial that we accurately track the numbers and structures involved. Artists deserve fair compensation for their cultural contributions, and we're here to make sure that happens. There's money at stake behind those rhymes, and we won't let it go unnoticed.

While major labels and platforms still hold significant influence in shaping the commercial direction of hip-hop, there are encouraging signs of change. Emerging venture players and the disruptive power of Web3 technology are opening up new possibilities for artists. To avoid repeating past mistakes, it is crucial to prioritize ownership of rights, foster collaborative relationships that nurture talent, and strategically diversify income streams.

The future of rap entrepreneurship lies in the fusion of streaming riches and blockchain innovation. This powerful combination has the potential to free artists from financial confinement and empower them to launch their own artist-owned companies. By closely examining the financial trends within the hip-hop industry, we can pave the way for architects and future generations to build sustainable wealth that uplifts communities.

The power of hip-hop extends beyond its beats and rhymes. It's crucial that the off-stage business dealings within the hip-hop industry bring empowerment, ownership, and equality. As MC Hammer warned years ago, hip-hop's impact cannot be underestimated. And now, it's time to ensure that hip-hop's money is untouchable too. Financial freedom is not just a desire; it's the future we must strive for. Let's seize this opportunity to empower ourselves through financial literacy and take control of our own destinies.

CHAPTER 5

BEYOND THE HYPE - BUILDING SUSTAINABLE HIP-HOP VENTURES

The allure of hip-hop stars securing that VC bag may make for enticing headlines. But when you dim the lights, the reality is that building sustainable businesses beyond the hype is a challenging grind. Managing expectations alone complicates life enough. Establishing strong foundations to weather industry storms? That's a whole different ball game.

Scaling too fast or neglecting the fundamentals can sink things faster than an unwanted diss track. The greats stand out thanks to their patience and vision. There are no shortcuts to crafting an empire. While people watch rappers-turned-entrepreneurs level up, it's the unseen work that propels them to the next tier. Those who are willing to put in the hours until the job is done will eventually reap mogul-level rewards.

In this chapter, we go beyond the captivating success stories of hip-hop businesses to uncover the essential foundations and strategic frameworks that ensure their long-term sustainability. Through meticulous analysis, we delve deep into building effective leadership teams, optimizing financial strategies, and adapting to ever-changing circumstances. Our goal is simple yet powerful - to provide a guidebook for transforming hip-hop hype into thriving enterprises and fostering stronger economies within our communities.

Weathering the Hype Storm

It's important for hip-hop startups to be patient and not rush their growth. Harvard Business School research says that in creative fields like music and fashion, it's crucial to balance early excitement with long-term plans. Instead of chasing short-lived trends or quick fame on social media, companies should focus on a sustainable vision.

This is even more important in the hip-hop industry, which can be unpredictable. Unlike tech industries with established ways of making money, hip-hop is still figuring things out. This puts pressure on hip-hop startups to seize every opportunity before things change. However, rushing without a good strategy often leads to failure.

Case Study: Kanye West's Past Miscues

If you take a closer look at Kanye West's ventures, you'll find a valuable case study that reveals the consequences of hype mismanagement on sustainability.

Back in 2011, Ye ambitiously expanded his fashion line beyond caps and tees, leveraging his influential cultural status and innovative designs. However, the rapid growth, coupled with Ye's perfectionism, led to distribution delays, manufacturing issues, and negative publicity during the early seasons.

In 2015, the fashion empire appeared to regain its momentum with inspiring global fashion shows and captivating store displays. However, personal challenges faced by Ye led to a series of setbacks over the next few years. Rushed releases, confusing branding, and inadequate quality control hindered his creative ambitions and failed to meet market expectations. By 2019, these inconsistencies caused the Gap partnership to stagnate and strained his relationship with Adidas.

Ye's ventures continually fell victim to the allure of hype, struggling to translate initial success into long-term sustainability. This serves as a valuable lesson - while hype may create opportunities, executing on those opportunities requires strategic thinking. Ye's once-magical touch quickly faded when obsession outweighed operational capacity.

This situation highlights the importance of organizational rigor in hip-hop ventures for maintaining commercial victories. Passion alone cannot withstand the demanding journey to stability. Mastering flashy marketing must be balanced with a vigilant CEO, a unified staff, and agile processes.

Establishing Effective Founding Teams in Hip-Hop Startups

When it comes to achieving long-term growth, having a strong founding team with diverse competencies is crucial for hip-hop startups. However, the spotlight often falls on solo artist-founders, overshadowing the collective efforts of well-rounded teams that bring different specialties to the table.

While it might seem like the famous star is the one doing everything, the truth is that it's the group effort that keeps the business going. We should start looking beyond just the big names like Rihanna and recognize the importance of having a team with different skills and experienced people.

Harvard research shows that hip-hop companies led by teams with various talents are valued 30% higher than those run by a single founder.

So, let's explore the optimal team structures that can propel hip-hop ventures towards success. By effectively deploying talent, these models defy the odds and pave the way for transformative outcomes.

The Creative Genius & The Wizard of Ops

Instilling originality and strategic thinking right from the start is vital to avoid stagnation. That's why pairing influential founder-CEOs like Kanye West or Jay-Z with strong operational partners like Marty Mensa and Juan Perez respectively has proven to be a winning formula for hip-hop startups.

This powerful combination allows for maximum creativity while also providing practical frameworks to turn ideas into action. It takes more than just a charismatic personality or a well-known brand to achieve long-term success.

Leveraging Specialists & Consultants

Beyond traditional leadership approaches, successful hip-hop companies go the extra mile by enlisting specialists in finance, technology, law, and growth strategy. These advisors play a crucial role in making informed scaling decisions and staying ahead of marketplace changes.

Take Dr. Dre, for example. He not only shaped Aftermath's remarkable music production through talented teams of sound engineers, visual directors, and marketing strategists but also made strides in the tech industry. Collaborating with Jimmy Iovine, he tapped into the expertise of software professionals to refine the Beats product vision and establish strong retail distribution.

By seeking out world-class talent beyond their internal teams, these firms avoid blind spots and ensure they stay at the top of their game. Opening doors to new opportunities also solidifies their reputation in the industry.

Artist Collectives Model

Alternatively, some hip-hop companies choose to center their operations around collectives that have risen together, standing the test of time.

The legendary Wu Tang enterprise maintains its edge through a vast network of interconnected members, studios, and affiliates that sustain their ecosystem. It's the combination of RZA's intellect, Method Man's charisma, Ghostface's street creativity, and Raekwon's business instincts that fortify their success.

By maintaining a tribe mentality, they not only foster longevity but also ensure that their output remains original and responsive to cultural shifts. The depth of creative inputs from various members and alumni keeps their work authentic and relevant.

Balanced Management Structures

No matter which model fits your company's vision, keeping a small and efficient structure is really important. In the hip-hop business world, having too many layers of management and confusion inside the company can slow things down. When there are too many levels of authority, it can lead to problems with communication and make it hard to support and develop talented people, which might make partners unhappy and leave the company.

To solve these issues, companies should follow the hip-hop mindset: keep trying, make things simpler, and get everyone moving together. Being open and not too focused on one central authority helps the company stay honest and lets teams work well even when things are tough. When everyone feels like they own a part of the company, it can inspire people to do amazing things, even when it seems impossible.

Optimizing Finances for Stability: Empowering Your Financial Future

When it comes to building a strong foundation, meticulous financial planning and cash flow management are essential. In the fast-paced world of hip-hop startups, however, funding needs and revenue projections can often be miscalculated during times of excitement and hype. This can lead to a harsh reality check down the line, crippling the execution of scaling plans.

But fear not! In this section, we break down effective strategies for optimizing your finances. From aligning with investors to implementing sound fiscal management practices, we provide you with the tools to ensure sustained operations and stability.

Crunch The Numbers - Forecast Properly

Financial forecasting is crucial to avoid unexpected setbacks that can derail your expansion plans. Don't overlook the essential funding needed for inventory, eCommerce platforms, tooling costs, and operational staff. It's easy for ambition to outpace financial means, leading to distress when capital runs dry.

Take the example of Frost of Ice, a jewelry startup backed by hip-hop manager Wack 100. They projected impressive monthly revenues after partnering with rapper 6ix9ine. However, they failed to account for manufacturing and shipping logistics, resulting in their closure within a year due to financial deficiencies.

By conducting meticulous pro formas and aligning spending with income expectations, you can prevent such pitfalls. Continuously updating your projections will also help you secure investor buy-in when more complex financing options like lines of credit become necessary.

Don't let your dreams fizzle out due to inadequate planning. Empower yourself through financial literacy and make smart decisions that will propel your brand forward.

Structure Optimal Investment Partnerships

Unlike tech verticals, hip-hop startups face unique challenges when it comes to securing capital. Historical investor bias has made navigating capital options a dilemma for these startups. However, there are strategies to optimize investment partnerships that align financial stability with founders' ownership values, reducing potential control issues in the future.

Bootstrapping

Leveraging personal capital through bootstrapping allows founders to retain full control and avoid premature external influence. Nipsey Hussle serves as an inspiring example by funding the initial production of Marathon store merchandise using his touring income and mixtape proceeds instead of seeking traditional startup capital.

However, it's important to acknowledge that bootstrapping can limit growth potential. Certain industries, such as tech platforms or retail chains with significant upfront infrastructure expenses, may require alternative sources of capital to scale effectively.

In order to achieve rapid growth, it becomes necessary to explore other avenues for funding. This is particularly crucial for businesses operating in sectors that demand substantial initial investments.

Remember, seizing these opportunities can be pivotal for expansion and success. By recognizing the need for alternative capital, businesses can position themselves on a path towards accelerated growth and industry dominance.

Angel Investor & Venture Capital Networks

Outside investors give money to help a company grow. But it can be tricky to find the right balance between letting the founder be creative and meeting what the investors expect.

Take, for example, Jay Z securing early-stage funding from Google Ventures for Tidal or Andreesen Horowitz betting on Sean Combs' vodka. When founders and investors see eye to eye, it usually leads to better results.

It's important that the artist's creative vision matches the investor's know-how while also keeping the artist in charge. To prevent conflicts in the future about different growth expectations, it's necessary to create plans for gradual growth that make both sides happy and keep the startups financially stable.

Revenue Share Models

Looking for a financing option that doesn't involve giving up ownership? Revenue share agreements with distribution and marketing partners might be the solution. These agreements provide non-dilutive financing while allowing you to retain control.

Here's how it works: Secure pre-paid inventory ordering financing from major retailers like Walmart or Target, leveraging future sales. Or strike content advance deals with streaming platforms like Netflix or Spotify to accelerate your work. The best part? If your projects underperform, there's no repayment required. Artists retain flexibility while still benefiting from financial support.

Crowdfunding Support

Finally, decentralization is revolutionizing hip-hop funding. Say goodbye to relying on traditional Silicon Valley gatekeepers. Now, creative projects can tap into Kickstarter-style modular capital through fan micro-investments.

Take Nas for example. His jewelry startup Hexclad received a whopping $40k in backing from supporters on the Republic crowd investing site. And here's the best part: these supporters get perks for their small dollar investments in the company. It's a true democratization of participation that honors community roots.

Financial Forensics - Track Key Performance Indicators (KPIs)

Once you secure the necessary funding, it's crucial to establish strict financial reporting practices. By shedding light on irregularities and ensuring expenses align with initial budgets, you can prevent unnecessary complications down the road.

Tracking the flow of money is absolutely essential. Without transparency and attention to detail, things can quickly spiral out of control. Uncontrolled spending can lead to major financial setbacks later on.

Regularly analyzing key performance indicators such as revenue growth, churn rates, and customer acquisition costs provides valuable insights into the efficiency of your business model. Identifying any discrepancies promptly allows for course correction and optimization of spending for maximum return on investment.

Maintain Mad Cash Reserves

Conservative cash planning is crucial for ensuring financial stability, even during uncertain times. By maintaining a healthy reserve of funds, businesses can navigate market fluctuations and maintain operations when faced with downturns. Stockpiling reserves not only safeguards essential functions like payroll, talent development, and R&D experimentation but also helps preserve trust among staff and prevents infrastructure setbacks caused by inadequate contingency planning.

Cash is the lifeblood of companies, and its absence can lead to detrimental consequences such as withheld salaries and shrinking resources. This erodes trust, diminishes momentum, and transforms employees into mercenaries. To ensure durability in the face of adversity, it is imperative to budget a sufficient operating runway of 12-18 months.

Optimize Cash Flow: Boost Receivables Efficiency

In the world of business, cash is king. That's why it's essential to ensure that receivables are promptly converted into cash. The smooth flow of capital keeps the wheels turning, but timely customer payments are crucial.

Remember the case of Diddy's Sean John empire? It faced a major setback when late payments from wholesale customers led to a failure in covering overdue manufacturing bills. The result? The business came to a screeching halt as working capital dried up. To avoid such damaging stalls, it's vital to tighten up your receivables process.

One way to safeguard your working capital is by structuring client contracts effectively. Strong legal terms can help prevent payment delinquencies. And if any issues do arise, resolving client disputes swiftly or exploring insurance options can help keep the cash flowing in. Don't let people get comfortable with owing you money.

Building an efficient receivables system is paramount for lean operations and continued success.

Learning To Pivot & Evolve

In the world of finance, lasting power lies not only in number acumen and team orchestration, but also in the ability to respond smartly to market fluctuations. It's about embracing an anti-fragile mentality that goes against the grain, allowing you to withstand external volatility.

Take a cue from hip-hop startups led by resilient hustlers like Jay-Z and Diddy. These entrepreneurs thrive by remaining adaptive, effortlessly navigating cultural shifts and changes in consumer demand. They embody hip-hop's creative spirit, making quick iterations based on real-life experiences instead of relying solely on data dashboards. Pivoting and flexibility are in their DNA, and it's a mindset that all ventures must embrace.

In this section, we delve into the essential mindsets and mechanisms that enable ventures to evolve smoothly when faced with market headwinds. Get ready to explore the strategies that will empower you to navigate challenges and seize opportunities with confidence.

Build an Innovation Culture

Unlock the power of innovation within your organization. Embrace the mantra of "innovate or evaporate" to eliminate stagnation and foster a fearless environment where bold ideas thrive, free from the fear of failure. Encourage employees to identify untapped opportunities before competitors do.

Leadership plays a crucial role in driving teams to take risks and push boundaries, rather than simply maintaining the status quo. Breaking free from repetitive cycles prevents fatigue among customers who crave surprise and delight.

To stay ahead, invest in ongoing research and development pipelines that enhance adaptability and fill gaps in your portfolio. Harness creativity to conquer unexplored territories in the marketplace.

Use the Rapid Prototyping Framework (RPF)

The Rapid Prototyping Framework (RPF) is a systematic approach for swiftly and efficiently developing and testing new product concepts. It involves creating small-scale prototypes to gather feedback and assess feasibility before committing to full-scale production. This approach prioritizes speed and flexibility in the product development process, enabling companies to iterate and enhance their products rapidly based on real-world testing and user input. The objective is to reduce the risk of costly errors and delays while expediting the introduction of innovative products.

By utilizing RPF, you can rapidly transform your novel ideas into tested products, gaining a competitive edge as an early mover. It also helps prevent expensive errors by allowing you to assess your product's market reception before mass production. This approach enables you to identify customer preferences and improve your product more efficiently. For instance, Beats Audio conducted trials with a few speaker samples before scaling up production, facilitating quicker product development. It's all about validating your concepts rather than relying on guesswork, leading to time and cost savings. Embrace the Rapid Prototyping Framework to expedite the success of your ideas.

Strategic Roadmapping: Meeting Success Milestones

In the ever-changing world of innovation, it's crucial to maintain agile and vibrant teams. However, having well-defined roadmaps as a foundation offers a strategic structure that turns research and development efforts into revenue-generating opportunities. These roadmaps act as a bridge connecting innovation and commercialization, providing stakeholders with a clear view of progress while allowing for necessary adjustments in response to market changes.

As Kanye West once said, "People get so caught up in trying to plan life out rather than just experience it. I make music for today, not tomorrow." While this original approach has driven his Grammy-winning hip-hop creations, adding structure and strategic direction can help avoid instability in business settings. Striking the right balance between flexibility and consistency is crucial.

Decision Making Delegation: Empowering for Success

Break free from founder bottlenecking issues that delay critical choices. By empowering trusted field experts to make decisions, you unleash the potential for rapid growth and development. Granting autonomy not only fosters leadership but also accelerates commercialization rates once market visibility improves. However, independent authority must align with overarching strategic principles.

Learn from Freeway Rick Ross, the legendary former Drug Kingpin who revolutionized decision-making in his crack supply chain. Recognizing the power of delegating authority, he empowered regional distributors to scale nationwide quickly and seize opportunities that a single centralized kingpin couldn't orchestrate effectively. By establishing guiding frameworks and deputizing reliable teams, Ross achieved unprecedented success.

CEOs, take note! Avoid cumbersome bureaucratic delays by delegating responsibility across specialized units like marketing, product, and tech. In a world with short consumer attention spans, quick decisions are key. Embrace delegation and conquer new heights of success!

Unlocking Success Through External Expertise

When it comes to strategic repositioning, seeking external counsel from specialists like venture capitalists and researchers is crucial. These advisors possess the knowledge to identify macro-level marketplace shifts and micro-competitive threats due to their wide-ranging business involvements.

By actively engaging with them, we can prevent tunnel vision and make informed decisions.

A Case in Point: Beats by Dre

Let's take Beats by Dre, for example. The founders, Dr. Dre and Jimmy Iovine, regularly sought guidance from tech private equity experts as they navigated the expansion of their music hardware and global distribution relationships in the era of digital streaming. By tapping into this external advisory network, they were not only able to increase market visibility but also enhance their brand valuation.

In today's rapidly evolving landscape, relying solely on internal perspectives may limit our potential for growth. By embracing external advisory, we gain access to invaluable insights that can shape our strategies and drive success.

Fluid Partnership Management: Navigating Win-Win Agreements

In the ever-changing market landscape, successful partnerships require adaptability and flexibility. This is especially true when it comes to high-profile retail partners, sponsors, and collaborators. By reevaluating and renegotiating terms, we can prevent fractures in these essential relationships.

Take, for example, Cash Money Records' groundbreaking distribution partnership with Universal in the early 2000s. Initially, traditional wholesale rates heavily favored the corporate side. However, through consistent success, Birdman was able to leverage his position and secure upgraded royalty tiers for Cash Money Records. This shift reflected a fairer profit-sharing model and helped prevent a talent exodus.

Outmaneuvering Crisis Moments

Hip-hop ventures face an ongoing battle to survive, despite their best efforts. Periodic demand contractions can pose a serious threat to solvency, putting these businesses in jeopardy.

While strategic foresight can help cushion against marketplace uncertainty, such as recessions, industrial disruption, and changes in client appetites, unforeseeable events still have the power to paralyze cash flow and leave businesses vulnerable.

In this concluding section, we delve into the crisis leadership principles employed by resilient hip-hop firms when navigating major storms. Discover how these savvy entrepreneurs weather the toughest challenges with resilience and determination.

Cutting Costs Without Sacrificing Quality

When quarterly sales are plummeting and visibility isn't improving, it becomes crucial to swiftly eliminate non-essential expenses. However, we must be cautious not to compromise on production quality. After all, shoddy craftsmanship can permanently damage our reputation.

The early 2020s global pandemic brought supply chain disruptions that tested many hip-hop fashion houses. To ensure longevity, savvy founders had to manage seasonal production budgets while facing acute revenue hits. The key was finding a way to decrease expenses without negatively impacting design capabilities. Ancillary expenses were strategically cut, leaving room for essential investments.

In times of financial uncertainty, it is imperative to make smart decisions that save money without compromising the excellence of our products or services. By carefully managing costs and maintaining a high standard of quality, we can weather any storm while preserving our brand's reputation.

Protection Against Fraud

In today's unpredictable landscape, organizations are constantly under threat from deceptive behavior that can suddenly disrupt stability. Even the most trusted employees and partners can succumb to temptation when oversight systems lag behind.

However, there are measures we can take to mitigate fraud and protect ourselves. By leveraging encryption technology, implementing robust reporting mechanisms, and conducting impartial audits, we can provide assurance and maintain integrity. This proactive approach is crucial in preventing major credibility damage.

A prime example of the devastating consequences of fraud is a case involving a well-known hip-hop artist's record label. In this instance, a trusted music producer embezzled millions from the label's bank accounts over several years to settle personal debts, pushing the company to the brink of financial failure. It serves as a stark reminder that small businesses, despite their promising beginnings, can crumble rapidly if internal theft goes unchecked. Safeguarding against fraud is paramount for long-term sustainability.

At its core, our commitment to ethics stems from the importance we place on customer trust. We draw inspiration from hip-hop's community roots in upholding honesty and integrity. By prioritizing ethical practices and staying vigilant against fraudulent activities, we preserve trust and ensure a solid foundation for success.

Insurance: Your Lifeline in Times of Crisis

Don't let unexpected disruptions bring your business to a standstill. With contingency capital solutions like business interruption or trade insurance, you can bridge temporary cash gaps and keep operations running smoothly until things normalize.

Take a lesson from the early days of Def Jam Records and its founder, Russell Simmons. When a devastating fire halted vinyl production in the late 80s, they relied on insurance payouts to stay afloat. These capital buffers proved crucial in overcoming unforeseen events that could have derailed the label's operations. Simmons didn't just bounce back; he emerged stronger than ever.

Insurance buys you time, ensuring that you have the financial support to navigate through challenging circumstances without closing shop completely. Premiums act as lifelines, providing stability when you need it most.

Customer Empathy & Adjustments: Building Stronger Relationships

In the aftermath of a crisis, genuine empathy can make all the difference in fostering goodwill and loyalty among customers. It's a powerful way for companies to recover faster and regain trust.

Take Diddy, for example. When Justin's Restaurant faced launch delays that led to a hit in reputation, Diddy stepped in with a thoughtful gesture. He offered free meals and Uber credits to customers, protecting their sentiment and strengthening the bond between them. Despite the initial hiccups, this move helped the restaurant overcome hardship.

After reopening, celebrity endorsements further propelled the locale into success. The combined efforts turned adversity into history, demonstrating the significance of customer empathy and strategic adjustments in achieving lasting growth.

Embrace Downcycles

Finally, don't shy away from slower periods. Instead, optimize your spending to future-proof your market position. Just like major sports teams rebuild to replenish their talent, hip-hop ventures should do the same.

Dip cycles offer a chance to transform your teams, systems, and offerings without facing the intense scrutiny that disruptions during growth phases bring. By reconfiguring these elements, you can prevent becoming outdated as consumer behaviors evolve and modernize your offerings. Embrace temporary shrinkage in market size through research and development and watch as it drives future revenue surges.

The Road Ahead - Building Hip-Hop's Business Legacy

In summary - In the world of hip-hop, there is a clear distinction between fleeting hype and solid institutions built to inspire communities for generations. Effective teams, sturdy systems, strategic planning, and adaptability during crises are what set these institutions apart.

The purpose of this chapter was to equip architects shaping the future of hip-hop businesses with proven frameworks. By identifying the core pillars of effective entrepreneurship within the hip-hop industry, we can strengthen its overall infrastructure. Imagine the positive impact on communities if hip-hop companies were known for their thoughtful craftsmanship and longevity, rather than flashy founders chasing quick success.

The culture surrounding hip-hop deserves economic opportunities that empower urban neighborhoods through employment, innovation, and role models who exhibit excellence. Just as rap collectives like Wu-Tang Clan and Native Tongue mesmerized the world with their transcendent creativity, there is potential for hip-hop entrepreneurs to elevate business to artistic heights as well. Let's seize this potential together.

Hip-hop hustlers have always faced challenges, but their imaginative spirit continues to drive them forward. They have paved their own way, creating opportunities through street smarts and raw awareness. It's time to nurture this spirit.

To unlock the true potential of hip-hop enterprises, we need to improve access to investment, business education, and policy support. By doing so, we can generate sustainable wealth on a larger scale. It's time for Fortune 500 boardrooms to embrace more diverse representation.

Financial fluency within hip-hop's creative circles will empower artists and accelerate their success. Let's build generational wealth that flows consistently, making it the norm rather than the exception. Imagine renowned hip-hop companies like Rocawear and Def Jam Records standing as institutions alongside Coca Cola and GE. It's time for hip-hop culture to shift from novelty to institution.

We have learned from past financial exploitation. Success leaves clues that can guide hip-hop builders in avoiding similar struggles in the future. By establishing stronger commercial foundations today, we can focus on influencing culture tomorrow.

Hip-hop has the power to reshape popular culture and uplift marginalized voices. Financial stability is crucial to ensure its enduring impact. Let well-run companies symbolize economic progress that benefits communities as a whole. Through this, hip-hop's imperative mindsets will continue challenging conventional norms across industries.

As hip-hop enters its next golden age, solving the right business equation today will create endless possibilities for tomorrow.

CHAPTER 6

BETTING ON YOURSELF - HIP-HOP CAREER STRATEGY BREAKDOWNS

Hip-hop is more than just music; it's a culture and a mindset. It embodies the ambitious hustler attitude, taking risks on one's own potential despite limited resources. Pioneers like DJ Kool Herc, Run DMC, and NWA have shown that fearlessly betting on your talents can lead to global success.

But the world of hip-hop is volatile, and artists must not neglect professional strategy. One hit single does not guarantee lifelong stability. While breakthrough moments captivate us, longevity in the industry requires understanding the business side of recording deals, touring, personal branding, investments, and Web3 channels.

In this chapter, we delve into tactical blueprints for various hip-hop occupations. We analyze the economic trade-offs across roles ranging from performers to producers and designers to agents. By examining career trajectory insights and real-life case studies, we aim to arm readers with financial literacy that empowers artists to back themselves. Let's explore models that optimize creative empowerment and wealth-building in the hip-hop industry.

The Hip-Hop Artist's Journey: Surviving An Ever-Changing Industry

Navigating the ever-changing music industry is no easy feat for hip-hop recording artists. They face immense challenges, from declining royalties to fleeting fame cycles and the pressures of physical and mental health. Shockingly, over 95% of these artists never achieve financial freedom solely through their art.

But there's hope. By understanding the modern career phases from startup to stardom, hip-hop artists can strategically navigate their way to success. It's time to examine tactical blueprints that will empower these artists to not just survive, but thrive in the long run.

Building Buzz - The Grind Phase

Gone are the days when simply signing to a label and getting an A&R assigned to your project could instantly launch a career. Today, independent artists must pave their own path to success before seeking partnerships. Welcome to the grind!

Building a strong foundation starts by attracting a core fan base through consistent content on streaming platforms and grassroots marketing. This phase of profiling often takes 1-3 years for most artists as they refine their style and songs. Patience is paramount, even in the face of tempting offers promising overnight fame.

Experts stress the importance of avoiding get-rich-quick gimmicks. True growth comes from focusing on the basics: creating amazing music and engaging with your online community. By nurturing loyal supporters who genuinely connect with your brand, you ensure long-term success instead of chasing fleeting popularity.

Take inspiration from acclaimed rapper Russ, who exemplifies the relentless hustle required in this industry. It took him five years from his debut to secure a major label deal by slowly converting his dedicated YouTube following into millions of mainstream fans through consistently delivering quality work and strategic online promotions.

Unlocking the Power of Digital Channels

Digital platforms offer limitless opportunities to expand your reach, especially during the crucial startup phase. By leveraging Instagram, TikTok, Fanbase, and Triller, you can directly communicate with your fans and weave captivating backstories into your content strategy. Plus, these channels provide monetization options through advertising shares.

Don't forget about Spotify! Uploading your music via Spotify Canvas increases its chances of being discovered through prime playlist placements. Distributors like CD Baby and TuneCore can also pitch your work to global platforms.

And let's not underestimate the power of YouTube. It's not just for music video premieres anymore. Engage your audience with creative vlogs that deepen their connection to your brand. Don't forget to include merchandise links for an additional stream of income. You can even tap into specialized niches by doing gaming livestreams.

Here's a fact: Artists who focus on developing their channels grow their fan base twice as fast as those who rely solely on music releases. Consistency in branding and meaningful conversations are key factors in converting followers into loyal fans.

Unlocking the Power of Touring

Touring becomes a profitable venture for artists when they have a dedicated local fan base of 5-15k monthly followers. This not only helps cover tour costs but also provides an opportunity to sell merchandise at shows. Opening for well-known acts in shorter sets can significantly boost their reputation, while collaborating with others allows them to gain more visibility. By using the earnings from shows to create more music and promote it, artists can achieve even greater success. So, if you're looking to make your mark in the music industry, building a loyal fan base and leveraging live performances is key.

Securing The Bag: Record Deals & Revenue Split Considerations

Labels are on the lookout for emerging talent with over 250k monthly listeners, ready to offer lucrative deals that can shape artists' futures. However, these deals come in various structures, making it crucial to navigate the intersection of creative control and opportunities with caution.

Let's look at the options available and see the money and creative compromises artists have to make:

Major Label Pipeline

Universal, Sony, and Warner are the powerhouses of the music industry, catapulting artists to stardom with their resources, promotional efforts, and quick routes to becoming a household name. But this success comes at a price. Newcomers are often tied down by lengthy multi-album contracts spanning seven years, limiting their creative freedom and ownership of their own recordings during that time.

However, there are some advantages. Artists who manage to avoid flopping can enjoy lucrative recording budgets, work with renowned producers, and receive marketing support for their passion projects. The major labels have nurtured global icons like Drake and Cardi B but few can withstand the grueling star-making machinery they operate.

Indie Label & Venture Partners

Mid-level music companies like 300 Entertainment and Alamo Records offer a unique blend of independence and institutional expertise. With these alternatives, artists can secure their master rights for 3-5 years while enjoying a fair revenue split of 50/50 after deducting expenses. Creative freedom is retained.

This hybrid model not only allows ownership but also provides backend participation for artists who achieve success. They aim to ensure transparency in royalty reporting to protect your interests. However, it's important to note that with less funding support, building awareness requires grassroots hustling unlike major labels. It's essential to fully leverage streaming and social media platforms to make an impact.

DIY Independence

Releasing music by yourself through online platforms gives you full control but means you have to pay for everything yourself. You won't have to share your earnings, but you'll need to be really good at getting fans and marketing because there's a lot of competition.

Chance The Rapper did this with his album Coloring Book. He used streaming platforms and bundled concert tickets to become a chart-topper. But doing it this way is hard and needs a lot of effort from you and your team (if you have one).

Web3 Direct Support

Crypto models change how music projects get funded by letting fans micro-invest and use smart contracts on the blockchain to distribute rights/royalties. Check out platforms like Royal, Opulous, and SongVest, that operate decentralized talent exchanges, eliminating middlemen and empowering artists to explore Web3 opportunities.

Navigating The Grind

Artists face a critical decision: indie creative freedom or major label amplification? It's a delicate balance that determines their long-term aspirations. Hybrid label collaborations offer flexibility, but they require proven ability to self-start. Navigating the trade-offs of independence, major, or hybrid will determine the trajectory of releasing music and its success.

But it doesn't end there. When Artist hit touring goals it also opens opportunities in acting, as well as other ventures like fashion, endorsements, and entrepreneurship, expanding their influence beyond just music. Today, artists must view music as interactive multi-channel entertainment properties, with touring sustaining their recording creativity in the long run.

It's time for artists to seize control and approach their craft strategically. The path to success lies in finding the right balance, embracing new avenues, and recognizing that the future is in their hands.

Maximizing Momentum: Achieving Long-Term Success

Once hip-hop artists achieve mainstream recognition, their focus shifts towards creating sustainable income streams that go beyond the temporary hype surrounding their albums. This involves harnessing the power of touring dominance, forming lucrative brand partnerships, exploring licensing opportunities, and embracing the potential of Web3 channels. The key to transforming fame into generational wealth lies in seizing the right opportunities before fading back into obscurity.

Let's examine options to leverage stardom and pave the way for long-term success:

Touring Until The Wheels Fall Off

Hip-hop artists are no strangers to the grueling world of touring. While streaming payouts may be meager, these artists rely on their concert runs as the primary source of income. They perform at concerts worldwide, sometimes doing 100 shows in a row, elite hip-hop stars like Drake, Future, and Cardi B continue to bring in massive earnings, averaging around $500k per night. And it doesn't stop there - VIP packages, clothing collaborations, and afterparty appearances all contribute to their tour revenue.

The financial rewards of rap touring easily surpass those from recording proceeds, with top acts making eight-figure paydays each year. However, this success comes at a price. The demanding travel schedules and back-to-back performances require immense stamina to prevent burnout.

In the fast-paced world of hip-hop touring, these artists truly go all out until the wheels fall off.

Maximizing Celebrity Branding

When fame strikes, hip-hop artists find another lucrative opportunity through sponsorships and endorsements. Consumer brands eagerly seek out these respected artists, offering seven-figure brand ambassador deals to tap into their social influence with young demographics. Rappers go beyond music, building personas that make them valuable partners for beverage, fashion, and technology companies. Their popularity translates into income-generating influence.

Mainstream Crossover Appeal

Expanding audience reach is crucial for sustaining marketing clout. It opens up exciting opportunities like film/TV collaborations and book publishing partnerships, allowing artists to diversify income streams during breaks from their music careers. By appealing to wider demographics, hip-hop artists can maintain relevance even after the allure of youth coolness fades away. Just look at Will Smith, who has epitomized this ability to forge long-lasting connections in Hollywood without ever fading into obscurity.

Catalog Monetization

Maximizing back catalog streaming royalties is crucial for veteran hip-hop artists, and it holds significant financial importance. With an astounding 550k new songs being released daily, the power of nostalgia becomes increasingly valuable.

In 2022, Meek Mill made a strategic move to boost his income by selling his catalog rights to Equity Distribution Holdings for a staggering mid-to-high 8 figures. And he's not alone in this venture. Post Malone and The Chainsmokers have also recently struck similar deals.

By owning their recordings long term, these artists can reap the benefits of asset appreciation and capitalize on the potential of their rights as platforms fiercely compete for beloved music catalogs. This presents a unique opportunity for strong yields and financial growth.

Direct Support Models & Ownership

Finally, web3 allows you to monetize your engaged fans directly, 24x7x365!

With the power of web3, artists now have the ability to leverage channels like NFTs to offer exclusive audio, art, and extraordinary experiences. But it doesn't stop there. Social tokens provide membership perks and even fractional song royalties. It's a game-changer.

Here are some web3 projects and Hip-hop stars who are taking advantage of them:

- Hip-hop NFT art/collectibles (Fetty Wap, Nas, Future)

- Pre-sale token access passes (Soulja Boy, Lil Yachty)

- Virtual performances in digital spaces like The Wave powered by Solana

- Song sales/distributions via platforms like Royal and Opulous

Transition to Icon

Hip-hop artists embody the essence of hustler versatility - their personas, lyrics, and bravado inspires fans while their success extends beyond music, solidifying their larger-than-life presence. But in the words of the Infamous Mobb Deep, "Survival of the fittest! Only the Strong Survive! To become an Icon, it takes strength and craftiness!

These living legends and iconic figures maximize their fame by consistently delivering impactful output and making calculated career adjustments. They not only survive market changes but thrive in them.

Hip-hop icons navigate and shape the industry with relentless determination. They use their status as a platform to make a lasting impact on society.

The Rise of the Rap Producer: Navigating Hip-Hop's Boom-Bust Economics

Step into the world of hip-hop icons and witness firsthand how they navigate and shape the industry with relentless determination. Discover how they use their status as a platform to make a lasting impact on society.

In the world of hip-hop, it's not just about the impressive lyrics and clever wordplay. Behind the scenes, there are unsung heroes known as producers who shape the entire sonic landscape of the culture. Yet, despite their indispensable contributions, producers face constant uncertainty in their careers.

This section delves into the challenges faced by hip-hop beat crafters, exploring ways they can navigate through unpredictable income fluctuations. By diversifying their skills and securing assets, these talented individuals can sustain their creativity while ensuring a stable financial foundation. It's time to empower producers to take control of their futures and thrive in this ever-changing industry.

Producer Purpose

In the realm of rap music, producers have a crucial role in shaping an artist's performance. Through drum patterns, samples, and instrumentation, they guide the cadence and create a rhythmic flow that captivates listeners. This requires not only strong musical skills but also technical expertise.

Legendary producers like Pharrell Williams, Jermaine Dupri, Metro Boomin, DJ Premier, and Dr. Dre have revolutionized the sound of hip-hop. Their innovative production techniques have pushed genre boundaries and left an indelible mark on the culture.

These pioneers have harnessed their musical prowess to redefine hip-hop for different eras. Their unique styles and signatures continue to captivate audiences with their undeniable influence.

Navigating Volatile Income Cycles

When it comes to rap producers, finding the perfect balance between artistic integrity and financial stability is no easy task. The unpredictability of royalties creates a rollercoaster of cash flow, despite the importance of their craft. To make matters worse, production fee-based models put pressure on them to constantly churn out content, leading to a cluttered industry. It's a constant battle that requires careful navigation and strategic decision-making.

Let's examine the volatile revenue drivers:

Beat Leases

Leasing copyrighted compositions to artists for a quick cash influx of $200-5000 may seem tempting, but it's a short-sighted approach. Unfortunately, this pay-and-go model offers no backend royalties from sales. To make matters worse, you would need an extremely high volume of leases just to break even, let alone turn a profit. Quantity over quality simply isn't sustainable in today's oversaturated market.

Don't fall into the trap of sacrificing long-term success for instant gratification. Rethink your strategy and prioritize sustainable business models that provide ongoing revenue opportunities.

Flat Fee Placements

Earning major album placements may seem appealing with temporary satisfaction and a short-term financial boost of around $15,000 to $150,000. However, relying solely on these front-loaded payouts can be misleading and ultimately fail to provide lasting security. It's easy to be seduced by the allure of quick money, but without recurring income streams, individuals may find themselves constantly searching for new opportunities instead of building a stable foundation for their financial future.

Royalty Splits

Securing backend royalty participation (20-50% production share) from breakout recordings is an alternative approach to ensure consistent income. It incentivizes the creation of timeless classics that outweigh quantity.

However, realizing royalty streams depends on unpredictable factors such as album rollout funding, release delays, and the fickleness of mainstream audiences. There are no guarantees that songs will translate cultural moments into commercial success. Additionally, the influence of record labels can diminish control.

This uncertainty makes relying solely on potential royalties insufficient for producers who need to juggle business obligations like studio overhead costs, equipment upgrades, and payroll. As a result, many find themselves tirelessly chasing individual payment cycles in a numbers game or even leaving the music industry altogether in search of more stable work opportunities.

Master Licensing

Licensing your full composition rights to publishers for upfront fees might seem tempting with larger instant payoffs. However, it's important to consider the potential long-term opportunity costs of forfeiting publishing streams. While it may offer a short-term solution, this approach can have detrimental effects in the long run. It's crucial to weigh the immediate gains against the potential losses and make an informed decision that aligns with your goals and aspirations.

Diversification Is Key

In the complex world of unpredictable opportunities, it is crucial to diversify your craft and revenue streams. Relying solely on one specialty is a risky move that leaves you vulnerable to fluctuating circumstances.

To navigate this challenging landscape, successful producers adapt and evolve. They become artists themselves, expand their songwriting skills, explore music ownership, and venture into multimedia platforms like scoring, NFTs, and podcast production. By embracing these diverse avenues of income, they achieve consistency in earning potential. The legacies of J Dilla and Pharrell serve as proof that this strategy extends the longevity of a career.

Furthermore, accumulating equity in your music assets allows you to benefit from the appreciation of rights over time. As catalog values increase through reissues, samples, and syncs, owning these rights ensures a secure source of passive income for the future.

Take control of your financial destiny by adopting a multifaceted approach to your craft. Through diversification and ownership of your creative endeavors, you can safeguard your financial well-being and thrive in an ever-changing industry.

Fostering Ownership and Freedom

For respected producers, creating their own independent label has long-term advantages that are different from their creative roles. Creative positions can become less important as musical preferences change quickly.

Becoming a founder and running imprints like Kanye West's G.O.O.D Music, Dr Dre's Aftermath Entertainment, and Pharrell's I Am Other not only protects prime earning years but also showcases promising next-generation talents. Streaming brings consistent label revenue and higher net income margins compared to outdated major label models.

Producers face income uncertainty, but they can secure stability by diversifying their skills and owning music rights. Being independent offers security and having a catalog of music ensures financial stability even in uncertain times.

Riding Hip-Hop's Managerial Wave: Guiding Talent in a Disrupted Industry

In the ever-changing landscape of the music industry, the role of hip-hop managers has become crucial in ensuring artist career stability. These innovative hybrid coach/marketers possess a unique skill set that allows them to navigate through turbulent times and protect financial freedom for their talent.

In this chapter section, we delve into the pursuits of these managers as they guide artists through challenging times and identify monetization streams that align with their creative impulses.

The Manager's Balancing Act

Hip-hop managers have a lot on their plate - they're not just handling creative feedback and tour logistics. They're also responsible for brand strategy, mental health support, and managing business affairs.

But the best hip-hop managers go beyond these tasks. They embody the core values of the genre, acting as amplifiers for artists while shielding them from the traps of the music industry. These managers prioritize creative freedom over financial gain.

Not all money is good money. The right managers filter opportunities to empower artists and help them retain control over their assets in the long run. Short-sighted decisions can damage trust, but those who are patient with their guidance will prevail.

Navigating Career Trajectories

When it comes to your career, having the right guidance is crucial. Trusted managers play a vital role in providing objective analysis and connecting you to the right opportunities, ensuring you avoid costly missteps along the way.

But their role goes beyond just that. They demystify those label offers, translating complex legal jargon and protecting your rights as an artist. In an industry where recording contracts still lag behind, these advisors serve as a shield against exploitation.

And it's not just about protection — they're also there to help you maximize your profits. With their expertise, they optimize touring revenue and bring clarity to financial matters, ensuring fair artist payouts and preventing shady deals with promoters that have plagued hip-hop talent for far too long.

Moreover, managers excel at fostering brand collaborations that align with your values. They know how to convert cultural influence into cash without compromising your integrity. While others settle for shallow endorsements, they aim for authentic partnerships that truly resonate.

In this fast-evolving digital landscape, exploring web3 technologies can be daunting. That's where your manager's close support comes in handy. They'll explain the dynamics and open doors to exclusive cutting-edge opportunities reserved for those in the know.

Today's top hip-hop artists need more than just social media managers. The complexity of the business demands trusted advisors who can balance creativity with commerce seamlessly. With their vision cultivation skills, they will lead you towards success.

Career Trajectory Insights

Navigating the manager hierarchy can be a complex journey, but certain milestones along the way can significantly enhance your credibility and propel your career trajectory. Let's explore these markers:

- As an entry-level manager, you'll support talent development, forge industry relationships, and earn around $50,000. Scouting remains crucial in this phase.
- After honing your skills and overcoming challenges, you can ascend to the middle tier of artist rosters, serving established niche musicians with earnings ranging from $75,000 to $125,000. This is where you can start claiming your stake in the industry.
- However, it's when you land a superstar like Nicki Minaj or Lil Baby—who dominate the top 30 Billboards—that the big bucks roll in. With commission percentages of around 10-20%, you can secure 7 figure salaries and attain elite status.

Demonstrating your smart management for independent clients can lead to big opportunities when celebrities seek your tactical skills. Having experience in artist and repertoire (A&R) work will give you valuable insights into artists.

Building strong relationships is crucial in this competitive field. Showcasing competence by avoiding mistakes like tour cancellations or bad brand associations is essential. Your career success depends on advocating for your clients.

Start this exciting journey with knowledge and ambition and make the most of every opportunity to create a successful career path for yourself.

Building Your Path to Ownership

As experienced managers move up, they often want to start their own companies. These companies focus on helping talented individuals they've supported in their early careers grow and succeed.

Quincy Jones, who established Q&A, played a pivotal role in elevating artists like Michael Jackson and Frank Sinatra to stardom. He used his visionary media knowledge to spot opportunities and negotiate favorable business deals. Similarly, hip-hop manager Chris Lighty propelled 50 Cent's rapid ascent and created Violator Entertainment, facilitating collaborations between artists like Busta Rhymes and Mariah Carey. Sadly, Chris succumbed to immense pressure and tragically passed away before he could maximize his full potential.

Today, managers such as Anthony "Top Dawg" Tiffith (TDE label) and Corey Smyth (Blacksmith Records) showcase a blended strategy by combining management and label roles. This integrated approach enables them to nurture up-and-coming artists, oversee worldwide music launches, and orchestrate prosperous tours. By retaining authority over different facets of an artist's journey, they extend an artist's career by ensuring structural ownership.

Paving New Lanes: Hip-Hop Venture Careers

Discover a hidden path in the hip-hop industry that goes beyond artistry. Unveiling an underpublicized avenue, we explore the world of business operational roles that support the expansion of the hip-hop ecosystem. While these unsung heroes may not have the same spotlight as flashy rap personas, they are the focused builders fortifying hip-hop's underlying commercial infrastructure.

In this insightful career overview, we explore the evolving landscapes within the thriving hip-hop industry, which is now valued at $30 billion. Discover the pivotal positions that offer the potential for a prosperous future, guaranteeing sustained success and expansion.

Fostering Startups

From bold indie labels to innovative streetwear brands and cutting-edge tech platforms, hip-hop startups need a diverse range of talented individuals who can lead the way in setting vision, executing strategies, managing finances, and driving growth. Key opportunities include:

Business Strategy

Commercial masterminds and creative consultants who comprehend nuanced marketplace dynamics connecting cultural influence to conversion. They design models and strategic plans crafted uniquely for hip-hop models beyond traditional constructs.

Finance & Analytics

A team of experts specializing in the unique financial landscape of the hip-hop industry. With in-depth knowledge and experience, they design custom forecasting models and reporting systems to navigate the variable income streams and early growth stages of this dynamic field.

But there's more work to be done. Music economics demands further examination, calling for the development of proprietary data that can unlock new insights and opportunities.

Marketing & Digital Branding

Hybrid Growth Experts who unlock the full potential of hip-hop projects. They play a crucial role in merging traditional strategies like tour and radio promotions with cutting-edge methods involving social media, playlists, and Web3 channels. This role demands a unique blend of analytical skills and creative thinking.

Operations & Supply Chain

Efficiently orchestrating the fast-paced world of hip-hop requires meticulous planning and precision. From navigating unpredictable hype cycles to managing the influence of celebrity endorsements, it takes skilled tacticians to oversee the intricate workings of manufacturing, distribution, and customer service for hip-hop brands to thrive on a large scale.

Technology Innovation

Web3 architects who truly understand cultural trends are paving the way for decentralized crypto models that will liberate hip-hop commerce from outdated frameworks. Say goodbye to the limitations imposed by the traditional music industry.

Investment Analysis

Delving into hip-hop asset classes like music rights, startups, and NFTs for seed and venture capital firms in pursuit of lucrative opportunities. This specialized field requires a deep understanding of critical factors such as streaming data, shifts in fan behavior, and intellectual property.

Admin & Team Operations

They are the driving force behind executive activities, seamlessly coordinating artist project communications, event planning, travel logistics, budget tracking, and vendor relationships. Their exceptional organizational skills keep the machinery running smoothly.

Legal & Business Affairs

They are specialist attorneys who navigate the unique deal structures in the hip-hop industry, including talent partnerships, licensing arrangements, and IP protections. Their role requires a combination of legal expertise and fluency in the world of hip-hop to prevent industry exploitation.

Artist Development

They are responsible for ensuring the mentorship and growth of the next generation of hip-hop talent. This involves scouting new talent, providing guidance in production and writing, and coordinating career development. Their role is vital in transferring hip-hop knowledge to rising generations, especially in the absence of traditional music education programs.

Hip-Hop Product Management

They oversee the execution of hip-hop art, whether it's recordings, films, books, or experiences. Their work involves collaborating with creators, blending project roadmaps with audience feedback, and requires an intimate understanding of cultural tastes and trends.

<u>The Road Ahead: Betting on YOU</u>

In conclusion, building a sustainable hip-hop career demands a deep understanding of modern dynamics and the use of tailored strategies to ensure longevity. Both artists and emerging entrepreneurs in the music industry face unpredictable paths, but by focusing on their core strengths and exploring diverse income streams, they can mitigate uncertainty.

The disruption brought by blockchain technology introduces new opportunities for creative funding and ownership, reshaping the balance of power. However, fundamental principles like engaging with loyal fan communities through authentic content and direct access remain essential for success. Building strong connections with fans can transform cultural influence into a steady source of income.

For those embarking on hip-hop careers, it's crucial to arm themselves with spiritual resilience, patience, and financial education before navigating the challenging terrain. Despite achieving mainstream success, the journey remains an uphill battle. Confidence in your talents and a willingness to collaborate can lead to historic achievements. Focus on planting seeds of creativity instead of chasing fame.

Now equipped with practical strategies and career insights, one question remains: Are YOU prepared to pave the way for the next generation, inspiring them and providing access to the hip-hop business? Can you transform your creative talents into community advancement? Just as Park Jams, open mics, and HBCU homecomings guided us through adversity, today's hip-hop underdogs need mentors to guide their journeys. Seize your destiny.

The time has come to transform hip-hop culture from an exploited novelty into an honorable institution. This transformation won't happen through complaints but through the execution of strategic career plans. Progress occurs when mindsets change, and knowledge is shared. Share these valuable insights as the fuel that aspiring entrepreneurs need to take flight. We all rise when we realize our potential power. Now is the era of independence and ownership. Have confidence in yourself and bet on your abilities first!

PART III: THE FUTURE

CHAPTER 7

WEB3, CRYPTO, AND NEW FRONTIERS

H ip-hop originated from visionary pioneers who embraced emerging technologies to amplify their voices and share their unfiltered artistic expressions. Whether it was cobbling together makeshift DJ setups or harnessing digital streaming for independent distribution, hip-hop's ability to adapt to technological advancements has become an integral part of its identity.

Now, five decades after its inception, hip-hop stands at the forefront of new frontiers anchored in decentralization. These frontiers offer fresh creative possibilities and commercial opportunities. Web3 and cryptocurrency promise unprecedented direct fan engagement, funding options, and ownership potential. Additionally, machine learning and AI open doors to interactive collaborations that were once unimaginable.

This chapter explores innovative new mediums, models, and technologies that intersect with hip-hop, fostering artistic freedom and financial security. The brilliant minds behind these scientific systems benefit from collaborative guidance, particularly from cultural custodians who understand the historical pitfalls of exploitation. Together, there are no limits to the empowerment that hip-hop can achieve by progressively merging art and science. The future is exceptionally promising.

Web 3.0: Platforms Designed for Fan Empowerment

While hip-hop pioneers skillfully navigated around obstacles in the music industry by leveraging emerging streaming and social platforms, the restrictive dynamics of Big Tech platforms have often hindered the full realization of creative potential and income security.

However, recently developed decentralized digital architectures aim to shift control back to community participants. They offer features like direct value exchange, rights verification, and collective governance, empowering fans and creators alike. This fan-centered approach aligns closely with hip-hop's core emphasis on amplifying the voices of the underserved.

In this exploration, we'll dissect the key components of this next-generation internet infrastructure known as Web 3.0 or Web3, and how it can promote artistic prosperity by enhancing independence and connectivity.

The Case for Decentralization

Industry analyst Cherie Hu succinctly captures the chaos affecting creatives by stating, "Multinational corporations continue to reap the most rewards from the exponential growth in music streaming revenues and the cultural impact of hip-hop, while superficial partnerships offer little financial benefit to artists beyond streaming royalties."

While social media and big tech have masterfully commercialized artistry, there has been very little modernization of the infrastructure to directly support creators, even though their works have generated billions for Silicon Valley giants.

Restrictive platform rules also limit full creative expression. For instance, TikTok has muted certain songs conveying protest messages, and YouTube's monetization algorithms have arbitrarily blocked hip-hop videos due to content filters. This economic censorship threatens the core purpose of art, which is to provide marginalized voices with outlets for truth.

However, emerging web3 companies like Royal, Audius, and Opulous are now enabling direct community ownership, seamless global exchange, and financial transparency, empowering creative autonomy. The era of entrenched gatekeepers is approaching its end.

Decentralization Explained

So, how exactly does the decentralized architecture empower artists and supporters? Let's break down the key components:

Peer-To-Peer Functionality

Legacy web platforms route interactions through centralized servers they own, making them vulnerable to censorship and third-party monitoring. Content removal and restrictions become common.

In contrast, web3 enables open peer-to-peer exchange of data, messages, and transactions without intermediary interference, thanks to advancements like IPFS and blockchain protocols. This prevents obstruction, allowing supporters to directly access artist content globally.

Creator Ownership & Control Through Tokenization

While social media platforms captivate users, they ultimately own all underlying data and content. Corporate control prevents fan ownership.

However, web3 enables creators to convert creative digital assets like songs, videos, and experiences into programmable tokens retained by artists. These crypto-backed assets verify rights protection for direct engagement with their community, unlocking new markets. Value goes directly to artists rather than Silicon Valley.

Direct Value Exchange & Participation

Currently, technology giants limit certain features and impose transaction fees, reducing artist revenue. They also use confusing and non-transparent algorithms to determine visibility.

Web3 cuts out middlemen by allowing smooth exchange of money, content, and opinions directly between users' wallets. Creators get paid directly, and users collectively decide how things work. This means feedback gets acted on fast without any red tape.

Improved Transparency & Trust Through Unchangeable Records

Currently, fans rely heavily on what artists and platforms tell them, lacking insight into the inner workings of business transactions, which makes them vulnerable to financial trickery. However, blockchains offer unchangeable, verified records that track transactions, including payments and ownership history. This transparency builds trust, strengthening the bond between artists and fans and preventing corruption in the industry.

Connecting Physical Experiences

While cryptocurrency features unlock new virtual possibilities, it's just as important to bring technological interactions into the real world. This can be achieved with innovations like NFC chips, which allow seamless acceptance of web3 assets and experiences in physical environments. For instance, wearable tech jewelry from CrowdPass turns concertgoers' phones into backstage pass NFC tokens, and Liverpool FC uses fan mobile wallets for secure ticketing. Widespread use of these technologies enhances the potential of web3.

Democratizing Community Controls

Unlike in social media, where decisions by individuals like Zuckerberg can shut down services without oversight, web3 users collectively manage platforms like Royal, Audius, and BitClout through voting. This ensures that the interests of the community are upheld and provides a system of checks and balances.

The Fan Empowerment Movement

In the end, web3 empowers the community by allowing direct access, open exchange, verified trust, secured rights, and participatory governance. Supporters become active contributors instead of passive bystanders. Gatekeepers no longer control attention through biased algorithms, and centralized authorities can't arbitrarily limit access to creative works. The focus shifts to supporter choice and creator rights.

Hip-hop, which celebrates artists from outside the mainstream or those representing marginalized communities, can help lead this change by educating people about the benefits of empowerment as web3 becomes more widespread. As Smokey Robinson once sang, nothing can halt this revolutionary movement, not even powerful tech companies.

Hip-Hop's Crucial Web3 Early Embrace

Given its independent spirit, hip-hop is revolutionizing the adoption of web3. By embracing decentralization, it breaks free from industry limitations and creatively engages supporters.

Investment in blockchain startups focused on music soared by 900% in 2021, surpassing $4 billion. Iconic artists like Nas, Nicki Minaj, and Snoop Dogg are joining this disruptive movement.

Now, let's delve into the early success stories of hip-hop in web3. Prepare to be inspired by the potential for empowerment!

Empowering Direct Supporter Participation & Ownership through NFTs

Non-fungible tokens (NFTs) are revolutionizing the representation of unique creative assets such as art, music, and videos. By minting these digital items on the blockchain, we can now establish limited ownership, enabling exclusive rights for exchange, appreciation, and exhibition that cannot be replicated by others.

In 2021, pioneering rap producer RAC took it to the next level by minting instrumental samples from his catalog as NFT collectibles. This not only created a reciprocal fan value beyond traditional streaming but also allowed supporters to own a share of his creative equity. As a result, RAC receives royalties from their participation. While this field is still emerging, its potential is incredibly promising.

Boosting Engagement with Social Tokens & Cryptocurrencies

Imagine having access privileges like early ticket allocations, merch discounts, and even creative input opportunities from your favorite rap superstars like Eminem and Nas. Well, thanks to personal exchangeable fan tokens powered by cryptocurrencies, this dream becomes a reality.

Fans can directly subsidize activities through crypto exchanges, unlocking incredible perks and influence in return. Artists are even running NFT presales where they accept cryptocurrency payments from fans who gain early ownership benefits such as exclusive audio leaks or profit-sharing arrangements as the asset value increases over time.

Unlock the Power of Decentralized Streaming & Music Rights Trading

Prepare to revolutionize the music industry with platforms like Royal, leveraging blockchain technology. Say goodbye to traditional labels and intermediaries as artists can now publish their music directly while connecting with fans through tokenized album copies packed with exclusive perks.

But that's not all. Royal's groundbreaking model ensures that artists receive 10-30% of streaming revenues and a majority share of album sales profits. Meanwhile, fans become active participants with governance votes and special access to virtual listening parties. Trust is built through transparent data practices.

But it doesn't stop there. With Royal, fans can even invest directly in songs they want released, while artists secure project funding in a transparent manner through smart contracts. It's a true partnership that bypasses industry gatekeeping, fostering creativity and empowering both artists and listeners.

Revolutionizing Entertainment: Virtual Concerts, Gaming & Metaverse Activation

Get ready for a mind-blowing experience! Thanks to crypto environments like Decentraland, hip-hop artists are taking their shows to the next level. Imagine attending a virtual concert where you can interact with other fans using avatars and VR interfaces. And that's not all – exclusive access passes in the form of NFTs unlock even more exciting content.

Snoop Dogg made history by performing a digitized show in The Sandbox metaverse. And he's not alone – big names like Offset, Quavo, and Lil Baby are immersing themselves in multiplayer gaming worlds like Fortnite, blurring the lines between the real world and the digital realm.

Revolutionizing Music Funding and Hip-Hop Startups

Say goodbye to outdated label constructs and predatory deals. With decentralized finance protocols and web3 models like Opulous, artists now have the power to access peer-to-peer capital from their engaged supporters. This means creative projects can come to life, with fans gaining fractional ownership and earning royalties through platform smart contracts.

But it doesn't stop there. Accredited investors looking to support hip-hop-related startups can now tap into the promising ecosystem with funds like North Island. This infusion of capital strengthens the infrastructure, fueling artistic progression and innovation.

Web3 is the catalyst that empowers hip-hop artists and fans alike, revolutionizing fan interactivity, career funding, and creative production. It's time to break free from external constraints and embrace a new era of prosperity in the music industry.

The Path Ahead: Web3 x Hip-Hop Collaboration

While still early, a thrilling partnership between hip-hop and technology is emerging in the realm of web3. The opportunity for both commercial independence and artistic innovation in the hip-hop industry is unparalleled. However, to maximize this potential, we must proceed thoughtfully and seek advice from those familiar with our culture.

We must remain grounded in our community's values. Rushing into the integration of advanced technologies without strengthening the foundation of hip-hop's business infrastructure poses a risk of startup failures. It's crucial that we establish partnership principles to protect our progress as we explore new territory:

1) Progress Over Hype

Don't get caught up in the hype of the crypto world. Instead, focus on fostering real and tangible advancements in culture. Take the time to build a strong educational foundation before diving headfirst into trendy crypto domains. Let's avoid jeopardizing communities that have historically been denied access by being patient and prioritizing education.

2) Pull Up Collectively

We can't afford to leave anyone behind in the web3 revolution. It's crucial that underrepresented populations fully participate and benefit from this new wave of technology. Collaboration is key to preventing the repetition of historical centralization exploitation. Together, we can ensure everyone has a fair opportunity to thrive.

3) Build For Generations

Let's think beyond temporary moments and create web3 models that are designed for communal transfer of knowledge, assets, and tools across generations. By focusing on purpose over profits, we can build systems that stand the test of time and serve our communities for years to come.

4) Strengthen Analog Foundations

Before we tokenize and decentralize hip-hop domains, we need to ensure that they have strong analog foundations in place. This means having proper legal protections, financing options, and systemic support that will enable sustainable ventures. We can only scale successfully in web3 if our infrastructure is solid.

5) Remain Open Source

Transparency is key to the success of our ecosystem. Let's keep documentation around technology building, deployment experiences, and exchange inventories open and accessible to all. This way, we can spread knowledge, empower individuals, and prevent any barriers or limitations from hindering progress in our decentralized journey.

The fusion of hip-hop's creative brilliance with web3's technological innovations will have a profound impact on the future of art. However, It's essential to prioritize the core principles of blockchain technology and underserved communities to guide mainstream crossover and prevent past divisions. The true ingenuity will flourish when education immerses all in its transformative power. Prepare yourself for exciting opportunities ahead.

Harnessing the Creative Potential of AI: The New Era

Alongside the rise of decentralized web systems, the swift progress in machine learning technology demands hip-hop leaders to skillfully handle upcoming changes as Computer-driven creativity unlocks new artistic possibilities.

Although AI offers a lot of opportunities to enhance hip-hop, It's crucial for innovative leaders to ensure that advancements are ethical and protect marginalized communities from the effects of biased algorithms from the past.

Let's explore these new areas together to assess risks, and seize the opportunities that await with the help of state-of-the-art machines.

Unleashing the Power of Creative AI

Experts boldly proclaim that "AI will be the defining technology of this generation," changing industries with automation and advanced decision-making. Amid these exciting developments, one area shines: AI's ability to unleash human-like creative genius.

AI excels in composing music, writing literature, crafting visual art, and creating multimedia. Platforms like OpenAI's Jasper and Claude surprise the literary world by generating original stories, song lyrics, and conversational prose (Written or spoken language that resembles natural conversation, often characterized by informal tone, direct address to the audience, and colloquial expressions.) Google's Magenta AI goes further, composing new instrumental music inspired by classic melodies.

In the visual realm, systems like NightCafe, DALL-E, MidJourney, and StarryAi turn text prompts into stunning illustrations at a rapid pace. Tech observer Ben Thompson notes the rising popularity of AI art, with early speculative NFT sales reaching high values.

AI adoption will transform hip-hop workflows, boosting efficiency and creativity. However, we must proceed cautiously to prevent commodification and erasure. Let's have a meaningful discussion about the path forward.

Implications on Music & Content Creation

The music industry is changing fast, and it's time to understand what's happening. With new technology like AI-powered apps and creative algorithms, hip-hop is exploring fresh ways to express itself.

Yet, important conversations about copyright, fair work, biases, and giving credit haven't been fully addressed. Rushing to use these tools without proper oversight could cause problems and ignore the importance of building a fair system.

For hip-hop, a genre born out of historical marginalization and exploitation within the industry, it's crucial to think about the ethics of using AI and making sure everyone benefits. Ignoring these issues risks repeating past mistakes.

But don't worry! There are ways to make sure things move forward positively:

Managing Creator Credits & Ownership

Make sure everyone gets fair credit for their contributions as collaboration between humans and AI becomes more common. Just like giving credit to skilled workers, we need to acknowledge the work of AI systems before it gets lost in commercialization. Use blockchains and tokenized receipts to track who contributed what, so it can't be changed later. Creating standards to protect against this is really important.

Creating Representative Datasets

Deep learning algorithms can learn a lot from data, but they can also pick up harmful biases if the data isn't diverse enough. For example, facial recognition AI often struggles with identifying people of color because they weren't well-represented in the training data. Being careful about how we collect and use data can help us avoid this kind of discrimination. The details of the data are crucial.

Ensuring Financial Accessibility

While some people dream of a future where AI helps everyone be more creative, many people still don't have access to basic technology because of differences in income and education. Making sure everyone has equal access to technology is really important before we rely too much on machines. When we all have access to the same knowledge, we can all move forward together.

Preserving Cultural Ownership

As we embrace new technology in creative fields like hip-hop, it's important to remember where we come from. By being aware of our cultural roots, we can make sure our traditions and values stay strong even as we use new tools. Let's ask important questions about inclusivity and make sure everyone's voice is heard as we shape the future.

The Road Ahead With AI

In short, generative AI has huge potential to change business and art in hip-hop. But we need wise leaders to guide this change for the benefit of everyone.

Resistance to change can hold us back, so finding a balance with innovative leadership is key. This balance will unlock a fair and abundant world where AI and hip-hop's spirit work together.

By embracing open machine learning with hip-hop's creativity, endless possibilities emerge. The future looks bright as pioneers lead the way.

CHAPTER 8

GLOBAL REACH AND CULTURAL IMPACT

Hip-hop, born in the Bronx and now a dominant $30 billion industry, has taken over the world with its infectious spirit and swagger. From developed to emerging markets, its global appeal knows no boundaries. In this chapter, we delve into key international regions where hip-hop has become a mainstream phenomenon, exploring how local artists have adopted their own interpretations that cross over to North American charts. This blurred line is a testament to hip-hop's universal influence.

By understanding these global dynamics, we can strategize sustainable expansion that maintains authenticity and avoids cultural appropriation. The international bag is overflowing with opportunities, but it requires careful attention to coherence. Let's survey the thriving global terrain of hip-hop together.

Hip-Hop's Commercial Impact: By the Numbers

Get ready to dive into the statistical landscape that quantifies hip-hop's global influence and immense commercial potential. The numbers speak for themselves:

- In 2022, hip-hop music surpassed a staggering valuation of over $30 billion worldwide. This includes revenue from recorded music, publishing, merchandising, endorsements, and touring.
- Experts predict that international streaming consumption will continue to grow at an impressive rate of 15-25% CAGR (Compound Annual Growth Rate.) in regions like Southeast Asia, South America, Africa, and China. This growth is fueled by the expansion of youth mobile penetration and the influence of endorsers.
- Hip-hop accounted for more than 25% of worldwide publishing royalties in 2021. PROs like BMI/ASCAP reported significant increases in backend songwriting copyright incomes, highlighting the global surge in sync and sampling.
- Domestically, hip-hop music festivals such as Rolling Loud attracted over 40% international attendees at flagship events. Additionally, global merchandising pop-ups have shown immense potential for monetization opportunities abroad.

The data unequivocally confirms what we already know - hip-hop is an unstoppable force that continues to strengthen its commercial dominance for decades to come. However, it is crucial that we have language and culture specialists who can translate local contexts to ensure continuity. Let's embark on a journey through these flourishing global terrains together.

Hip-Hop Hotbeds: Thriving Global Scenes of Musical Influence

While hip-hop's roots can be traced back to the Bronx borough of New York City, it has since blossomed into distinct regional movements with fervent followers and unique sub-genres that shine a light on local dialects and experiences.

Let's dive into some standout international hip-hop hotbeds that have nurtured stars who not only conquer the North American mainstream pop charts but also captivate global audiences beyond their native borders.

United Kingdom

Experience the explosive rise of the United Kingdom's hip-hop scene. Artists like Stormzy, Skepta, Dave, and Central Cee have garnered attention for their energetic performances and thought-provoking messages.

Known as "grime," these acts blend dancehall, electronic, garage, and hip-hop, creating a unique sound that captivates audiences. With freestyle battles and intense lyricism, the scene thrives in London and beyond.

What sets grime apart is its raw storytelling of street life and societal issues that resonate not only within the UK but also across the Atlantic. Tracks from these artists climb the American rap charts while they regularly tour stateside.

Skepta's Mercury Prize-winning album Konnichiwa and Stormzy's historic achievement as the first grime rapper to top UK charts have opened doors to TV appearances and festival opportunities worldwide. It's no wonder that front man Damon Albarn of Blur hails rap music as the new punk rock for this generation.

France

In France, hip-hop thrives with vibrant representation from North African and Caribbean communities. This multicultural fusion has birthed a captivating movement that transcends generations, blending languages and global sounds seamlessly.

From MC Solaar's pioneering work in jazz-infused hip-hop to modern trap sensations like Niska, Dosseh, Naps, Jul, and Gazo dominating pop charts both in France and former colonial regions such as West Africa and Algeria – French hip-hop showcases unparalleled stylistic versatility.

Bilingual rappers are credited with revolutionizing French lexicons through their inventive use of slang in hip-hop. Their ability to capture youth fascination has even earned Drake an ambassador nomination from President Macron.

Collectives like PNL and SCH have emerged from humble beginnings outside Toulouse to build devoted followings. These artists achieve diamond-selling albums, blockbuster tours, and even fashion labels without relying on mainstream media – proving that authenticity triumphs.

Since 1981, public radio station Funky Souls has been dedicating itself to broadcasting French hip-hop. This long-lasting support helps propel the scene both nationally and internationally, creating enduring momentum.

Germany

Germany has carved out a distinct lane for hip-hop, embracing unknown artists and fostering their success. Since its overseas expansion in the early 80s, Germany has become a hotbed for engaging voices in the genre.

Artists like Advanced Chemistry, Fantastischen Vier, Sammy Deluxe, and Culcha Candela paved the way with provocative content and ground-breaking sounds that continue to inspire contemporary German rappers.

Today, hip-hop reigns as Germany's most dominant music genre, accounting for over 20% of national music market revenue. The acceptance and influence of hip-hop bloom across the country.

Exciting newcomers such as badmómzjay, Luciano, and Nimo are rapidly gaining recognition by addressing topics like feminism, mental health, and political participation. Their multilingual rhyme schemes and profound songwriting elevate German hip-hop's impact on a global scale – streaming platforms are spreading their influence far and wide.

While exporting German hip-hop remains somewhat limited due to the dominance of English-language pop charts worldwide, strong touring circuits, branding opportunities, and labels like BMG provide stability for artists' careers within Germany. The scene continues to mature with a resilient spirit that guards against fleeting trends.

Nigeria & Ghana

Experience the vibrant hip-hop scene of Nigeria and Ghana! With youth making up nearly 70% of the population, these West African countries are embracing globalization and mobility, resulting in a diverse range of hip-hop representations. From Afrobeat hip-hop hybrids to chart-topping singles and viral dance crazes, the influence of Nigerian and Ghanaian artists is crossing borders and making waves worldwide. Witness the power of music as it bridges ethnic groups and fosters creative communities anchored in fearless expressionism.

South Korea

Discover the unstoppable force that is South Korean hip-hop culture. Blending rap dexterity with pop melodies, cinematography, and unwavering work ethics, K-Pop superstars like BTS, Blackpink, EXO, and Zico have achieved unprecedented international success. Breaking records on global charts and captivating audiences with their mesmerizing performances, they prove that language barriers can be shattered when talent meets innovation. Prepare to be amazed by the phenomenon that has taken the world by storm.

Australia

And finally down under - Experience the rebellious spirit of Australian hip-hop. Defiant rappers like Iggy Azalea, The Kid LAROI, and MattyBRaps are gaining recognition on a global scale by channeling raw emotions and candid songwriting that resonates with outsiders everywhere. Breaking through Grammy nominations for Rap Album/Song categories, they showcase Australia's contribution to the international hip-hop scene. Get ready to dive into a unique blend of North American influence, cultural similarities, and distinctive Australian sounds that will leave you wanting more.

Embark on a journey through three continents where hip-hop knows no boundaries. Immerse yourself in the beats, lyrics, and stories that transcend languages and cultures. Discover how different countries shape this ever-evolving genre while leaving an indelible impact on its listeners worldwide. Open your mind to new perspectives as we celebrate the universal power of music.

Global Consumption Case Study: BTS Achieving International Hip-Hop Success

BTS's journey to fame in the United States and their collaborations with rap stars like Megan Thee Stallion offer valuable lessons in global promotion strategy. Let's look at key points:

Compelling Visual Storytelling

Their music videos blend captivating choreography with emotional acting, grabbing attention in today's short-attention-span era. They invest over $2 million in each video.

Effective Social Media Engagement

Regular vlogs give fans a peek into the band's life, building strong connections beyond just music. They use global hashtags and engage with fans regularly.

Language Adaptation

They started with Korean-only tracks but now include English verses, making their music more accessible internationally. Their lyrics resonate with audiences worldwide.

Recognition and Collaboration in the US

They appear on late-night talk shows, perform at major award shows, and grace magazine covers like Vogue and Rolling Stone, gaining visibility. Collaborating with artists like Halsey and Nicki Minaj adds credibility.

Innovative Business Model

Their Weverse app allows direct communication between artists and fans and integrates with their global online shop. This modern approach reaches fans anytime, anywhere.

Combining Music with Activism

Their UN speeches showcase their social awareness, attracting new audiences beyond just pop music fans. Their meaningful message resonates.

Long-Term Cultural Impact

Their blend of English rap and pop solidifies their place in culture, ensuring lasting relevance.

Promoting Cultural Impact Responsibly

As hip-hop gains global popularity, it's crucial to focus on ethical localization and attribution to maintain integrity. Let's carefully cultivate global ecosystems as interest grows abroad. Measure carefully before expanding.

Rethinking Cultural Appropriation

This section emphasizes the need to carefully consider how we develop global ecosystems as interest in hip-hop grows worldwide. It's important to think carefully before expanding too quickly.

While some critics criticize international music styles like K-Pop/Afro-fusion as cultural appropriation, sociologist Dalton Higgins argues that this view is oversimplified. He suggests that in today's interconnected world, cultures often mix and exchange ideas naturally. This view emphasizes the exchange of ideas rather than appropriation.

Higgins and others suggest that artists like Zico from Korea pay homage to hip-hop pioneers like Tribe Called Quest and Outkast, who themselves drew inspiration from global music. Now, genres blend together as artists from different regions collaborate, creating new and exciting sounds. This cultural exchange benefits everyone involved.

Building an Inclusive Infrastructure

No matter how you look at it, supporting international hip-hop artists requires sustained management and marketing efforts to ensure long-term success beyond just one hit single. Labels like Nigeria's Chocolate City and Canada's Ovo Sound understand the importance of providing media training, tour planning, and legal support to artists abroad, helping them grow at their own pace and avoid common pitfalls.

It's crucial to include marginalized communities in the spotlight and ensure they have equal access to opportunities.

Understanding Local Context

As hip-hop's popularity grows worldwide, it's essential for artists to understand the social, political, and economic nuances of different regions to avoid cultural missteps. Geopolitics and diplomacy play a significant role in today's entertainment landscape, requiring influencers to be culturally literate.

Investing in Community Wealth

Instead of just criticism, it's important to invest in local communities by supporting projects like youth music programs, small businesses, and affordable housing. This reciprocity helps sustain positive cycles of growth and ensures that everyone benefits from hip-hop's success.

The Future of Global Hip-Hop

In conclusion, hip-hop's worldwide expansion is connecting people like never before, surpassing boundaries of religion and politics. As internet access grows, hip-hop's popularity will continue to soar, but we must be mindful of preserving identity and avoiding exploitation.

With careful planning, hip-hop can empower marginalized voices and challenge oppression on a global scale. Their stories deserve to be heard, and their potential deserves recognition.

Imagine a world where everyone is connected and free to express themselves. This is the essence of hip-hop's impact.

As hip-hop crosses oceans, success should be measured by how many creators feel empowered to share their truths through their art, even if it starts locally. Artistic freedom is paramount.

If the next era of international hip-hop focuses on equity, accuracy, and inclusivity, then chart success and business ventures become less important. What truly matters is the joy and connection fostered within the community.

Let's celebrate our diversity and the history of hip-hop that has brought us to this moment. The world is waiting for our anthems, and now is the time for creativity to shine brightly.

CHAPTER 9

KEEPING THE BEAT - SUSTAINING HIP-HOP'S LEGACY

For 50 glorious years, hip-hop has thrived, its beats pumping like a vital life force through our speakers. From humble Bronx block jams hosted by DJ Kool Herc to streaming platforms reaching billions worldwide today, this genre keeps our hearts beating to its rhythm.

But beyond its commercial success lies a deeper calling — protecting the creative spirit that makes hip-hop urgent and empowering for marginalized communities who birthed this art form in search of representation and upliftment. To ensure its authenticity remains intact and prevent cultural displacement, we must pass the torch of stewardship from one generation to the next.

In this chapter, we'll explore how hip-hop can move forward and become even more vibrant. We'll discuss building community connections, opening up opportunities, and ensuring that the pioneers of hip-hop are financially supported. Let's look at ways to empower this beloved genre.

Honoring Hip-Hop's Resilient History & Origins

Before we discuss how to keep hip-hop alive for the future, let's honor those who started it all despite facing tough times. These pioneers faced difficulties with determination, creating the amazing culture we love today. Remembering their struggles is important, as the saying goes, "Those who forget the past are doomed to repeat it."

Indeed, hip-hop started as a way to have fun and forget about tough times in the Bronx during the 1970s. But we shouldn't overlook the incredible bravery it took to create it. People faced tough challenges every day, just trying to get by and make their communities happy. These struggles are often forgotten, but they're what made hip-hop great.

DJ Kool Herc remembers those tough days well: "We didn't have much back then. My sister Cindy and I made shirts and sold them locally to save up for records and audio gear for our block parties." Being resourceful was key before big companies got involved.

Just like blues came from the pain of slavery and gospel rose above Jim Crow laws, hip-hop also flourished boldly despite generational poverty caused by the mistreatment of minorities during the American apartheid era. Early rap songs told stories of resilience to maintain dignity in tough times.

Just as bebop and R&B pioneers kept innovating in cramped nightclubs during segregation, hip-hop DJs created new music by looping percussion when they didn't have full instruments. Cultural creativity really came from facing oppression.

Let's recognize pioneers like Kool Herc, Afrika Bambaataa, Grandmaster Flash, and Grand Wizard Theodore — they crafted a new musical world from overlooked vinyl and rundown infrastructure in the Bronx. Their bold creativity gave birth to beloved hip-hop, but many today forget the poverty and struggle that inspired this ingenious DIY spirit.

As OG rapper Melle Mel proclaimed back in his pivotal 1982 song "The Message" - "Don't push me cause I'm close to the edge. I'm tryna get over." This firsthand experience conveyed important messages from the streets, keeping early hip-hop authentic — going beyond entertainment to resonate with the people. Vulnerable activism mattered more than catchy tunes.

While later generations have been fortunate to avoid the hardships faced during hip-hop's early days, remembering the exact origins and neighborhood conditions that sparked its inventive spirit preserves its cultural essence as it spreads globally. The integrity of this genre depends on it.

Preserving Hip-Hop's Guiding Principles

Afrika Bambaataa, known as the Godfather of hip-hop, promoted the "Each One Teach One" philosophy, encouraging sharing knowledge among elders, peers, and youth to nurture artistic growth. It's crucial to revive this belief for a sustainable future.

Early hip-hop wasn't just about entertainment; it aimed to uplift spirits and raise awareness among forgotten communities, helping them overcome challenges.

Hip-Hop historian and Cornell professor Jelani Cobb examines six core pillars guiding hip-hop's emphasis on community advancement historically beyond just music including:

1) Political Activism & Civic Engagement

2) Entrepreneurship & Financial Empowerment

3) Social Cohesion & Collective Economics

4) Cultural Integrity & Afrocentric Pride

5) Public Health & Self Care

6) Futurism & Technological Literacy

As later generations pursued materialism and superficial fame, they lost sight of hip-hop's deeper purpose. Returning to the foundational values of hip-hop strengthens its spiritual essence, benefiting people in profound ways. It's about prioritizing purpose over personal gain.

Sharing Truths is Essential for Passing the Torch

Contemporary elders like Rakim, KRS-One, Public Enemy, Salt N Pepa, MC Lyte, and Roxanne Shante are touring and sharing their stories through intimate lectures. This exchange of truth is crucial for passing on the torch of hip-hop's legacy. We need these figures to safeguard the essence of hip-hop before corporate interests overshadow its soul.

Encouraging veterans to write memoirs, like Jay Z's "Decoded" and LL Cool J's "Finding Your Winning Rhythm," helps share spiritual insights and preserve cultural values for newcomers who may lack context from viral TikTok videos. Education lays the groundwork for creative innovation across generations.

Additionally, practical discussions about both the positive aspects and potential pitfalls of the art form are essential for helping emerging artists navigate the challenges that come with fame and the pressures of the entertainment industry. There's a lot more to consider beyond just the music itself, and addressing these topics is crucial for preparing artists to face the challenges ahead.

The Bridge Aint Over (KRS-ONE Voice)

Imagine modern cyphers where veteran hip-hop icons collaborate with the new generation, bridging the gap between eras. Picture legendary artists like Rakim, KRS-One, and Black Thought hosting talent showcases, offering feedback to up-and-coming rappers in weekly sessions on platforms like Twitch or TikTok. The potential for merging different generations of talent is endless.

Finding ways to avoid creative stagnation is a significant challenge, especially when nostalgic tours might restrict artistic development. However, embracing innovative approaches like Web3 models enables the sharing of insights and creative participation across generations. This can involve using digital twin avatars, NFT songwriting prompts, AR concert experiences, and extended reality role-playing adventures. These technologies allow for the infusion of old-school values into ongoing artistic endeavors, ensuring that both traditional and modern approaches can thrive together.

Imagine a Fortnite-style multiplayer universe where Hip-Hop fans can choose between veteran Golden Era MCs like LL Cool J or Rakim and contemporary artists like J Cole and Drake. They then compete in a rap battle royale game judged by virtualized Hip-Hop legends. This creative virtual experience monetizes nostalgia in an innovative way.

Archiving Hip-Hop's Cultural Artifacts

Apart from passing down guiding frameworks across generations, it's vital to physically preserve significant hip-hop cultural artifacts. This ensures proper historical context as the genre evolves into various styles and sub-genres. Let's explore the institutional support needed to maintain this crucial heritage.

The Universal Hip-Hop Museum

Emerging as arguable hip-hop's most ambitious endeavors in hip-hop archiving is The Universal Hip-Hop Museum. It's spearheaded by legendary rap impresario & former president of Def Jam Recordings Rocky Bucano and esteemed hip-hop journalist Nelson George.

Containing over 300,000 physical artifacts including photography, magazines, concert fliers, vinyl records, street fashion, and fine art, this extensive $150 million bricks-and-mortar shrine is designed by renowned architect Sir David Adjaye, known for his work on the National Museum of African American History in Washington DC. It will provide education on the regional stylistic evolution of hip-hop across each US coastline.

The museum also tells the story of hip-hop's five core elements' origins through multimedia exhibits, including special performances and public panels. This ambitious project solidifies hip-hop's status as an esteemed American institution.

The Hip-Hop Hall of Fame & Museum

The Hip Hop Hall of Fame, established in 1992 by James 'JT' Thompson, has been a cornerstone of hip-hop culture, commemorating its legends and contributions. Initially conceived to be funded by Hip Hop Hall of Fame Awards TV Shows, its plans for a physical museum faced setbacks due to industry conflicts, delaying its realization until recent years.

Presently, the Hall of Fame operates from its Harlem headquarters, with plans for a museum and hotel complex in New York City's Midtown Manhattan facing political hurdles. However, the organization's vision expands beyond traditional spaces, with plans for innovative ventures such as the Hip Hop Hall of Fame Cafe & Museum in Atlanta, Georgia, featuring TV/Film studios, and retail stores in various cities.

Additionally, the Hip Hop Hall of Fame continues to engage audiences through radio shows, awards ceremonies, and a cutting-edge metaverse experience, ensuring the culture's preservation and evolution.

Expanding University Archives

Ivy League universities like Harvard and Cornell are also expanding their archives to include hip-hop histories. They are collecting items like vinyl records, notebooks, costumes, and art to preserve legacies for future generations, ensuring that the contributions of originators endure even after they are gone. Digital databases are also being used to share this knowledge widely.

These growing academic collections enable upcoming cultural scholars and artists to grasp the intricate dynamics that led to the birth of influential subgenres. They document key singles and trendsetters objectively, avoiding relying solely on personal anecdotes that may distort facts. Accurate documentation is essential for preserving history, even as the intrigue of unknown details persists.

Web 3.0 Community Collections

Decentralization also offers a chance to celebrate hip-hop history through digital platforms in the metaverse, where artifacts are digitized using blockchain technology to create Non-Fungible Token collectibles. These tokens showcase unique and rare items, ensuring they cannot be forged.

Picture having virtual graffiti pieces created by the pioneering subway bomber Skeme displayed proudly in your personal virtual space. Or owning limited edition breakdancing sneaker NFTs that grant access to exclusive Bronx cypher footage. Digital permanence is ensured through blockchain technology, supporting hip-hop's remarkable rise in archival form.

Financial Stability For Hip-Hop Legends

Unfortunately, many respected elder statesmen of hip-hop, like Grandmaster Flash, Kurtis Blow, and Ultramagnetic MCs, face financial struggles in their later years, despite their ongoing influence on the genre. Implementing reforms in royalty distribution and establishing philanthropic support systems could help provide proper care for these pioneers, acknowledging their significant contributions, which are often overlooked as attention shifts towards new trends. It's essential to discuss infrastructure changes to address this longstanding community issue.

Snoop Dogg and 50 Cent have quietly donated money to various rap legends who have faced financial or physical challenges over the years as revealed by Snoop during an appearance on the All The Smoke podcast. While they prefer to keep these acts of philanthropy private, their contributions have provided much-needed support to elder statesmen of hip-hop who may have fallen on hard times. This includes offering financial assistance to artists in need without seeking recognition for their efforts, exemplifying a commitment to supporting their fellow pioneers in the industry.

Despite Snoop Dogg and 50 Cent's commendable philanthropy towards struggling hip-hop veterans, their efforts highlight a systemic issue within the industry. While their actions exemplify the importance of supporting elder statesmen, it also underscores the lack of a structured support system to ensure that these pioneers receive the care and assistance they deserve without relying on sporadic acts of generosity from fellow artists.

Advocating For Better Streaming Royalty Payouts

Persistent activism aimed at dismantling archaic streaming royalty payout models is crucial for ensuring viable lifelong incomes for hip-hop creators. This effort goes beyond addressing terrestrial radio royalty reform, which historically denied equitable pay for Black artists, as highlighted in a 2016 letter to Congress signed by Jay Z, Beyoncé, Usher, Robin Thicke, T.I., and others. By advocating for fair compensation from streaming platforms, hip-hop artists can secure financial stability both retroactively and in the future.

Nonprofit organizations like the Black Music Action Coalition are actively pressuring legislative bodies to demand improvements in Spotify and Apple Music streaming models. Their aim is to raise artist royalty rates from the current average of \$0.0033 per stream to levels closer to equitable label parity, which could reach around 15%. This advocacy seeks to ensure that hip-hop artists receive fair compensation for their creative work in the digital streaming era.

This advocacy is especially crucial for older hip-hop acts who rely heavily on catalog streaming, as they may not have access to the lucrative revenue streams from touring and merchandise. Ensuring fair compensation through streaming royalties becomes vital for maintaining their dignity and financial stability as they continue to contribute to the cultural landscape.

Direct-Support Community Fund Models

Encouragingly, decentralized Web 3.0 crypto models are facilitating direct patronage exchanges, bypassing corporate intermediaries. Platforms like Royal are pioneering the Hip-Hop Legends fund, enabling everyday fans and emerging artists to directly sponsor royalty streams for seminal architects like Rakim. This ensures their rightful financial freedom in later years and supports emerging MCs who inherit stylistic blueprints. This grassroots equity model is shaping the future of hip-hop support.

Imagine token-gated hip-hop metaverse experiences where supporters globally immerse themselves in firsthand backstories through intimate VR cyphers with icons like Nas, honoring their immense but often economically undercompensated contributions in laying artistic foundations. These digital channels democratize access, preserving legacies while empowering fans to directly support their favorite artists.

Managing Music Rights within the Hip-Hop Community

Nonprofit initiatives such as HipHopDX's collaboration with the Web 3.0 music rights management platform Royal are pioneering communal ownership of the publishing catalogs of deceased hip-hop legends. This innovative approach ensures sustainable incomes for artists' families in the long term, akin to the successes seen with the Marvin Gaye estate, thus preventing destitution while preserving invaluable creative intellectual property.

Archie Davis, founder of Royal and former Luminary Media CEO, articulates their ecosystem infrastructure's goal as providing transparency, access, and monetization capabilities to the hip-hop community, particularly artists and fans who have shaped the culture over the past 50 years but have not always received fair financial compensation. This alignment of intentions toward justice can pave the way for impactful solutions.

Fostering Hip-Hop Education To Cultivate Next Generation

As hip-hop becomes increasingly dominant among the Gen Z demographic, it's imperative to enhance music and cultural education to align with the genre's ethos and support its economic ecosystem. However, the current educational landscape often falls short in adequately incorporating hip-hop into curricula. To address this gap, initiatives should focus on integrating hip-hop into school programs, offering courses that explore its history, cultural significance, and socio-economic impact. Additionally, providing resources and training for educators to effectively teach hip-hop-related subjects can ensure that future generations receive a comprehensive understanding of the genre's contributions to society and its potential for sustainable growth.

Closing Hip-Hop Music Education Gaps

Despite hip-hop's indisputable status as America's most influential music genre over the past 50 years, its urgent early origins stemming from the economic challenges of 1970s Bronx, which exposed the devastating impacts of post-industrialism on impoverished inner-city communities, are often overlooked in public education and collegiate music business programs nationwide.

For instance, music academics Dr. Sonia Tetlow and Dr. Brian McLaughlin underscore the "shockingly low statistical coverage hip-hop receives across performing arts curriculums in public schools or college music business programs," despite its significant global economic impact and consumption. This oversight jeopardizes the comprehensive understanding of hip-hop, relegating it to nostalgic triviality rather than recognizing it as a respected American classical innovation that empowered the oppressed through artistic brilliance.

Advancing Hip-Hop Business Training

The absence of financial and entrepreneurial education tailored to the unique nuances of the hip-hop industry, including artist development, touring, streaming strategies, crypto models, and experiential productization, remains glaringly scarce within current business school curricula. This gap persists despite over 50 million Americans engaging in creative pursuits full-time within the booming gig economy. It becomes imperative to innovate curricula to address these deficiencies and provide comprehensive business training for aspiring hip-hop professionals.

Although there has been a commendable expansion in overall music business academic coverage over the last decade, with renowned undergraduate programs available at institutions like Berklee, NYU, and UCLA, there remains a disproportionate lack of focus on niche areas tailored to rap artists, hip-hop producers, and DJs. Operational models, copyright frameworks, and career roadmaps specific to these segments of the industry lag behind despite the significant commercial footprint of the hip-hop genre. This gap warrants attention and efforts to develop specialized education in these areas within music business programs.

Unlocking Access To All

Even before high school, budget cuts to creative programs like sports, arts, and music due to pandemic measures risk limiting opportunities for lower-income kids. This makes it harder for them to explore their talents. It's important to fix this issue quickly to keep hip-hop thriving and accessible to everyone, so creativity can keep growing across generations.

Realigning institutions with hip-hop's diverse socio-economic roots is crucial for ensuring its sustainable future. Without proper support, there's a risk of losing the essence of hip-hop as charismatic stars retire. We need to nurture the next generation of lyrical talents, music producers, fashion innovators, graffiti artists, and dancers to carry on the legacy seamlessly.

Solutions To Catalyze Sustainable Future

To catalyze a sustainable future for hip-hop, several proactive measures can be implemented. Firstly, integrating hip-hop music and culture into formal education curricula from youth programs to college courses ensures consistent exposure and understanding across all levels. Creating credential pathways specific to hip-hop education allows aspiring artists and professionals to pursue structured learning and career development. Additionally, establishing community touchpoints that bridge the gap between educational institutions and the professional world strengthens continuity and support for hip-hop culture beyond fleeting mainstream trends. These measures collectively fortify the foundation of hip-hop, ensuring its longevity and cultural significance.

Highly encouraging template blueprints now exist to strengthen hip-hop infrastructure:

- Implementing Hip-Hoponomics in High Schools and Colleges. Hip-Hoponomics: How to Empower Urban Youth with Financial Literacy & Entrepreneurship Through Hip-Hop is a groundbreaking guide that harnesses the cultural resonance of hip-hop to teach financial literacy and entrepreneurship to urban youth. This book outlines a dynamic curriculum that blends hip-hop culture with essential financial education, offering practical strategies for educators and administrators to engage students. Through the exploration of hip-hop's history, analysis of lyrics, and case studies of successful artists and entrepreneurs, it aims to empower young individuals with the tools for financial independence and disrupt the school-to-prison cycle. **Hip-Hoponomics** is a call to action for using education, culture, and community to inspire change and unlock the potential of urban youth.
- Afterschool programs like "Hip Hop Sustains," led by hip-hop pioneer Kurtis Blow in Harlem, are coaching foundational DJ and Music Production skills, paving the way for the next generations. This grassroots knowledge transfer proves foundational.
- Nonprofit organizations like the Hip Hop Architecture Camp, administered by the prestigious Columbia Graduate School of Architecture, deliver pivotal STEM exposure by marrying hip-hop culture with tactical community infrastructure improvement initiatives in historically oppressed neighborhoods often denied public investment. Beyond just dance and graffiti, expanding the scope to include elements like entrepreneurship and solution design thinking broadens the understanding of what constitutes the true hip-hop ecosystem. This approach allows greater

opportunities for participating youth to take ownership, overcoming disenfranchisement through applied focus areas like Urban Planning and Civil Engineering.

- Venture talent accelerators like Andreessen Horowitz's Cleo Capital actively fund emerging hip-hop-focused startups such as Lyric Financial. These startups provide literacy tools and access to business capital for new artists and diverse founders who have historically faced discrimination from traditional financial institutions.

- Several reputable universities now offer Hip-Hop Studies degrees as bona fide academic concentrations, including McNally Smith College of Music, the University of Arizona, and the University of Calgary. These programs grant scholarly credentials that allow graduates to leverage their cultural fluency in securing ventures and operational roles. They contribute infrastructure support behind the scenes through areas like A&R, Marketing, Content Production, Tour Management, and Creative Technology.

Additionally, Howard University, a historically black college, led the way by offering the first Hip Hop-specific class to students in 1991. Since then, colleges across the United States, including prestigious institutions like Harvard, Penn State, USC, UCLA, Stanford, Rice, Duke, Princeton, and NYU, have introduced various courses focusing on Hip Hop culture. In 2012, the University of Arizona introduced the first interdisciplinary Hip Hop studies minor in the country. McNally Smith College of Music in St. Paul, Minnesota, has offered a diploma in Hip Hop studies since 2009, emphasizing music technique, production, and industry economics. Tiffin University in Ohio began offering a music performance degree with a focus on emceeing and beatmaking in 2013. Recently, the London College of Music started offering a BA (Hons) degree in Hip Hop

Performance and Production, covering MCing, DJing, producing, and recording. In addition to classes and degree programs, the field has seen growth in conferences, symposiums, readers, anthologies, and institutions like the Hip Hop Archive and Research Institute at Harvard. As of 2017, the top universities to study Hip Hop at were McNally Smith College of Music, North Carolina Central University, and the University of Arizona.

In a full-circle moment, Howard University, the first to offer hip-hop specific classes in 1991, has achieved another milestone with the establishment of the Warner Music/Blavatnik Center for Music Business in 2021, made possible by a generous $4.9 million donation. This remarkable achievement underscores Howard's commitment to fostering excellence and equity in the music industry.

Leading this transformative initiative is Jasmine Young, an esteemed alumna of Howard University with deep ties to hip-hop culture and extensive experience in management, marketing, and education. Her journey began at Def Jam Records shortly after graduating from Howard University in 1994. There, she supervised artists like Jay-Z, DMX, Erick Sermon, and Onyx, while also overseeing joint venture projects such as Roc-a-Fella Records and Ruff Ryder Records. Rising through the ranks, she eventually became the senior director of marketing and general manager of rapper DMX's Bloodline Label, where she made significant contributions to the company's success.

With Young's appointment as director of the Warner Music/Blavatnik Center for Music & Entertainment Business at Howard University, a new chapter in hip-hop education begins, highlighting the importance of investing in the next generation of music industry professionals. Her extensive experience and commitment to giving back underscore the significance of mentorship and training in shaping the future of the music and entertainment industry. Through initiatives like the fellowship program and engaging programming for students and the broader community, the center aims to prepare diverse talent for management careers in the music business, ensuring a vibrant and sustainable future for hip-hop and beyond.

Once adequately resourced, this combination of early-stage creative exposure, credentialed undergraduate pathways, startup launching support, and alumni professional development opportunities for hip-hop-obsessed students creates an indispensable pipeline sustaining cultural ownership and career self-determination long-term.

The achievements yet to come are bound to be astonishing. Now is the moment for unified action, transforming hip-hop from a passing interest into an esteemed lifelong calling, with abundant opportunities accessible to communities historically excluded from fully engaging in the music industry. The doors are open—step through them boldly!

PART IV: BUILDING WEALTH

CHAPTER 10

CHARTING YOUR BLUEPRINT - DEFINING THE VISION

The quote "If you fail to plan, you are planning to fail!" attributed to Benjamin Franklin, resonates profoundly within the context of hip-hop's evolution and its pioneers' achievements. The genre, born from the crucible of creativity and struggle, has always been more than just music; it's a movement defined by resilience, innovation, and the relentless pursuit of success. Hip-hop's architects, through their enterprising hustle and unparalleled creative flair, have not just transformed the music industry; they've influenced fashion, language, art, and entrepreneurship, fundamentally altering the socio-economic landscape of their communities.

The journey of hip-hop from the streets to global stages underscores the importance of detailed planning and strategic envisioning. The pioneers of hip-hop actualized their game-changing revolutions not solely through raw talent but through meticulous plotting and a visionary approach. They understood early on that to translate far-flung ambitions into tangible outputs, it was crucial to visualize the outcomes and meticulously work towards them. This forward-thinking mentality enabled them to navigate the challenges of their environment and leverage their art to create opportunities not just for themselves but for their communities as well.

This strategic approach to creativity and business within hip-hop culture exemplifies the essence of Franklin's words. By planning their paths with precision and purpose, hip-hop's pioneers were not merely avoiding failure; they were architecting their success. Their stories teach us that outcome visualization is not just a practice but a catalyst that transforms dreams into reality. It highlights the power of intentionality in the creative process and the entrepreneurial spirit, reminding us that behind every groundbreaking achievement lies a blueprint of foresight, planning, and unwavering determination.

As hip-hop stands at a pivotal juncture, determining its destiny beyond the confines of mere entertainment, it beckons its architects to delve deeper into the essence of their intrinsic motivations. This critical introspection is not just about understanding personal drives but about re-envisioning hip-hop's role in shaping culture, influencing societies, and forging pathways to financial independence for its practitioners and followers alike. The journey ahead requires a compass that is forged from introspective vision, one that can guide hip-hop into its next golden era—an era that promises to maximize cultural impact while securing financial freedom for its community.

This chapter seeks to explore and articulate frameworks that are essential in optimizing the creation of your blueprint for success within the hip-hop domain. It's about recognizing the power of hip-hop as a force for positive change and leveraging it to open doors to abundance for many. The goal is to not only manifest wealth in the monetary sense but to enrich the cultural, social, and intellectual tapestry of our communities.

We'll dive into strategies that empower individuals to harness their unique talents and visions, aligning them with broader societal needs and aspirations. From understanding the dynamics of the music industry to leveraging technology for brand building, from harnessing the narrative power of hip-hop to advocate for social justice to fostering entrepreneurship within the community, this exploration is comprehensive. It's about crafting a narrative that is authentic, impactful, and liberating.

This is a call to manifest afresh, to reinvent and reinvigorate the spirit of hip-hop. It's an invitation to contribute to a movement that goes beyond beats and rhymes, to a cause that is about uplifting and empowering. By investigating these frameworks, you're not just plotting a course for personal achievement but are participating in the collective effort to guide hip-hop towards a future that celebrates creativity, champions social equity, and ensures economic empowerment for its creators and aficionados alike.

Let's embark on this journey together, with the wisdom of the past lighting our way and the boundless possibilities of the future as our destination. The blueprint for the next golden era of hip-hop awaits—let's manifest it with intention, innovation, and integrity.

Defining Personal Missions - Legacy beyond Music

Leaving a legacy beyond music dives deep into what makes hip-hop truly impactful, going beyond short-lived streaming fame to create a lasting influence on culture and society. It prompts aspiring artists and industry stalwarts alike to delve deeply into their core purpose, urging a reflective journey to understand not just the 'what' and the 'how' of their craft, but more importantly, the 'why' and the 'for whom'.

Cultural historian Jeff Chang's insight underscores the necessity of examining one's motivations and the impact of their art as the cornerstone for building a career that extends beyond the realm of music into lasting influence. This chapter challenges individuals to pause and consider their broader mission, advocating for a foundational approach where music serves as a medium for a more significant message and mission.

The pursuit of notoriety and the allure of instant gratification through digital platforms, while tempting, are juxtaposed against the enduring fulfillment derived from creating art with intentionality and purpose. It's about crafting a narrative that not only resonates with audiences on a superficial level but also engages them in deeper, more meaningful ways. This reorientation towards understanding and defining personal missions is presented as a crucial step for anyone aspiring to leave a legacy that transcends musical achievements.

By knowing oneself and one's intentions, artists can chart a course that aligns with their values and aspirations, ensuring that their journey in hip-hop is not just about commercial success but about making a lasting impact. It's about envisioning a legacy that contributes to the culture, empowers communities, and inspires future generations.

This chapter is an invitation to reflect, to redefine success in broader, more impactful terms, and to pursue a path in hip-hop that is as rewarding personally as it is beneficial collectively. Through introspective questioning and a commitment to a mission that goes beyond music, artists are guided towards creating work that not only stands the test of time but also elevates and enriches the lives of those it touches.

Creating a Lasting Impact: Envisioning Your Unique Legacy

It's time to deeply consider how your work can leave a meaningful mark. To do this, ask yourself some critical questions:

Identifying Your Cause: What are the specific issues you want to address through your work?

Representation and Access: Which underserved group can benefit from your voice and how can you make a difference for them?

Positive Influence: In what ways can your work uplift people's spirits or change their thinking for the better?

Beyond Music: Aside from music, what other forms of media can you use to share your message?

Collaboration for Greater Impact: Who can you partner with to strengthen your impact and further your cause?

Inspiration and Resilience: What keeps you motivated and passionate about your projects, especially during challenging times?

Understanding your deeper purpose, beyond just fame or chart success, helps you create work and business strategies that align with your personal goals and support your community over time, even when fame comes and goes. Having a clear vision helps you stay focused through tough times.

Before chasing fame and streams, first engage in deep self-reflection. Seek meaning beyond music, defining success in more substantial terms. Remember Steven Biko's powerful words, "The most potent weapon in the hands of the oppressor is the mind of the oppressed." With liberated minds, dare to dream boldly!

Reverse Engineering The Future

The power of starting with your ultimate purpose and working backwards to create a roadmap of key milestones is one of the best ways to manifest your mission. This approach ensures your efforts are aligned with your long-term goals rather than being swayed by short-term distractions. By envisioning where you want your career to be in five years, you can set clear, incremental goals to guide your journey. These might include:

- Increasing music sales and streaming numbers.
- Growing your social media following and improving engagement.
- Boosting live performance opportunities and touring fees.
- Enhancing your financial stability through total assets and scorecards.
- Forming strategic business partnerships.
- Achieving personal satisfaction and lifestyle goals.

This method helps prevent the common pitfall of veering off your desired path by chasing superficial successes defined by others. With a clear, self-defined direction, you're better equipped to navigate the challenges of the entertainment industry with confidence and purpose.

Activating Allies & Advisors

It is important that you incorporate insights from a variety of mentors and advisors as you work towards your milestones. These individuals can provide crucial guidance, help you stay on track, and offer the diverse perspectives needed to navigate the complexities of your journey.

However, it's essential to be mindful of the pitfalls of seeking advice that only validates your preconceived notions, as this can lead to missed opportunities for growth and necessary pivots. To avoid the trap of confirmation bias, actively seek out and thoughtfully consider a wide range of viewpoints.

Here are several types of advisors worth connecting with, each offering unique forms of support, insights, and accountability to enrich your career path:

Industry Veterans are seasoned professionals with a deep understanding of your field, providing insights into its history, trends, and strategies for success. They guide you through the industry's complexities, offering valuable advice on making informed decisions and navigating challenges.

Creative Mentors are artists or creatives who share your vision and can offer constructive feedback on your work. They help you hone your artistic expression and develop your creative projects further.

Financial Advisors are finance experts who help you with budgeting, investing, and managing your earnings for long-term stability and growth.

Legal Counsel are lawyers knowledgeable about your industry who provide advice on contracts, intellectual property, and other legal issues to safeguard your work and interests.

Marketing Strategists are professionals who assist in shaping your brand, enhancing your online presence, and planning how to effectively reach your target audience.

Life Coaches are individuals dedicated to personal development, guiding you in balancing your career goals with your personal well-being and fulfillment.

Peer Mentors are fellow artists or entrepreneurs at a similar career stage, providing relatable advice, mutual support, and accountability.

Technology Consultants are experts on the latest tools and platforms, helping to boost your creative output and make your operations more efficient.

Engaging with a mix of these advisor archetypes ensures a well-rounded support system that can guide you through the multifaceted aspects of building a successful and fulfilling career. Each brings a specialized set of skills and perspectives that, when combined, can significantly enhance your ability to make informed decisions and effectively execute your comprehensive career blueprint.

Specifically, as it relates to launching or enhancing your Hip-Hop career these specific advisors can take your game to the next level:

The OG Mentor

Experience the wisdom of seasoned hip-hop legends who blazed the trail, facing the same challenges you now encounter. These OG mentors offer invaluable firsthand advice to build your confidence, unleash your creativity, and navigate the gritty realities of the industry.

Their battle-tested playbooks, extensive networks, resilience in the face of adversity, and invaluable insights will fast-track your career and shield you from rookie mistakes. The access they provide is truly priceless.

But remember, respect their time and expertise by offering reciprocal value. Leave entitlement behind and remain humble and hungry at all times.

The Master Teacher

Learning from industry giants like Shanti Das, Pierre "Pee" Thomas, and Courtney Stewart is crucial for anyone aiming to succeed in the hip-hop arena. Shanti Das, a former Executive Vice President of Urban Marketing and Artist Development at Universal Motown Records, has a rich history of managing marketing campaigns for artists such as Akon, Erykah Badu, and Ashanti. Her expertise in navigating the music industry's complexities makes her insights invaluable. Pierre "Pee" Thomas, the CEO and co-founder of Quality Control Music, has significantly influenced the rap and hip-hop scene, contributing to the rise of major artists. His visionary approach to artist development and music production offers a roadmap to success. Courtney Stewart, known for managing Khalid and his roles in record label operations, tech investments, and philanthropy, exemplifies the diverse skills needed in today's industry.

Seeking mentors of their caliber can dramatically propel an aspiring artist or executive's career. While formal apprenticeships with these veterans may not be available, emulating their strategies and learning from their experiences can provide aspiring talents with a significant advantage. Their collective wisdom on marketing, branding, and strategic partnerships is a testament to the power of combining creative talent with business acumen, offering a blueprint for success in the competitive music landscape.

The Vision Cultivator

Advisors like manifestation coaches and creative thinkers who help artists think beyond the usual limits of the music industry are vital when tapping into your higher realm. They use techniques like imagining future successes, tapping into spirituality, and relying on gut feelings to break free from traditional career paths. These advisors encourage artists to follow their own unique direction instead of seeking approval from others, leading to a more authentic and fulfilling career by unlocking their true potential.

Figures like Eric Thomas, known as the hip-hop preacher, have made significant strides in bridging the gap between spirituality and the competitive worlds of sports and music. His unique approach to coaching has resonated with many in the music industry, offering a blend of motivational speaking and life advice that draws heavily on hip-hop culture. Eric Thomas's work exemplifies the powerful impact of combining spiritual guidance with practical life skills, further illustrating the wide array of resources available to artists seeking to cultivate a richer, more balanced approach to their careers and lives.

Moreover, as the author of this book, I, Ash Cash, have also played a role in being a vision cultivator for hip-hop artists. Through my teachings that "Abundance is Their Birthright," I have dedicated myself to guiding artists in managing their lives and finances more effectively. My approach emphasizes the importance of mindset, financial literacy, and self-empowerment, drawing from my own experiences and insights to inspire artists to achieve greater success, both personally and professionally.

While the idea of spiritual advisors in hip-hop might seem unconventional, it's not uncommon among artists seeking deeper fulfillment and guidance. Icons like Jay-Z have openly acknowledged the positive impact of spiritual practices on their lives and careers, highlighting a broader trend within the industry. When he said, "Uh, we gon' reach a billi' first. *I told my wife the spiritual s#%! really work.* Alhamdulillah," he was professing his goal to become the first hip-hop billionaire—and it came to pass.

Many hip-hop artists have sought wisdom from figures such as The Honorable Louis Farrakhan and Bishop T.D. Jakes, among others. These spiritual leaders offer perspectives that often contrast with mainstream industry advice, providing artists with insights that nurture their personal growth and creative expression. This blend of spirituality and mentorship enriches the artists' journeys, allowing them to navigate their careers with a sense of purpose and integrity that transcends the conventional paths to success.

Together, these examples highlight a growing movement within the hip-hop community towards embracing a more holistic, spiritually grounded approach to career development and life management.

The Connector

The Connector refers to highly connected culture enthusiasts who operate at the intersection of various industries, including entertainment journalism, talent management, and venture capital. These individuals offer invaluable resources such as exposure, project financing, marketing, and digital expertise, effectively bridging opportunities across sectors. However, it's crucial to carefully vet these connectors to ensure they adhere to ethical consulting practices and proactively protect your interests. To avoid exploitation, prioritize aligning your values with theirs from the outset, ensuring a partnership that supports mutual growth and respect.

The Support Circle

Never overlook the importance of your inner circle—those close to you who offer personal feedback that goes beyond business, ensuring your mental health and inspiration remain intact as you chase ambitious career goals over the long term. This support network is crucial for maintaining your spirit's buoyancy and well-being.

As your vision becomes clearer, having a trusted council to provide guidance is essential. Such advisors ensure your progress is protected through accountability and help illuminate your blind spots, proving invaluable as you aim to reach your goals more efficiently. The key is to activate all these support systems wisely, leveraging their diverse insights and support to navigate your path successfully.

Conducting Competitor & Market Analysis

Beyond the invaluable process of inner reflection and consulting with wise mentors, understanding the current landscape of your industry, including the forces of competition and broader market opportunities, is essential. Conducting thorough analysis enhances your situational awareness, enabling the creation of strategies that stand out and endure over time. Sun Tzu's adage, "Know thy enemy and know yourself, and you need not fear the results of a hundred battles," underscores the importance of this comprehensive awareness in navigating the complexities of the modern business environment.

By examining the details of the current market and understanding the positioning and tactics of competitors, you can navigate your career or business ventures fearlessly, armed with the knowledge to make informed decisions and execute plans that lead to sustained success. Let's delve into the intricacies of the modern business landscape, preparing ourselves to maneuver through challenges with confidence and strategic foresight.

Analyzing the Competition

While obsessively comparing oneself to peers can lead to resentment, smartly analyzing the career paths of contemporaries can provide valuable insights that help distinguish your own path. Keeping an eye on the competition helps avoid the trap of becoming a copycat and losing ambition. For instance, observing the innovative steps taken by industry leaders like Jay Z, who is developing a blockchain music rights exchange, or Cardi B, who is expanding her fashion empire, can reveal unexplored market niches or additional services that fans desire but are currently overlooked. Such creativity leads to unique, uncontested market moves.

Applying academic models, such as Michael Porter's "5 Forces Analysis" from Harvard, can also shed light on potential threats to your revenue streams, ranging from the clout of rival artists and the influence of major labels in streaming, to alternative entertainment options vying for the youth's attention, like gaming and Web 3.0 metaverse experiences. A comprehensive analysis provides a richer understanding of the situation, enabling a more informed strategic response. This knowledge is particularly empowering for underdogs, helping them overcome disadvantages and succeed in a competitive landscape.

Investigating Market Trends

Exploring different research areas like music futurology, youth ethnography, and global trend forecasting helps identify new opportunities in the music industry before they become too common. For instance, in-depth trend analysis from organizations like Stylus, Semiocast, and Fancensus back in 2015 could have identified the growing interest in emo-rap and the shift of Gen Z towards multimedia streaming platforms well before these trends became mainstream in 2020. Recognizing such trends early on can lead to successful market entry, capturing fan interest before it peaks.

Rather than following the latest fads, like those often seen on TikTok, a thorough analysis of market trends can guide the creation of unique products and identify untapped areas for innovation. Success lies in predicting where future opportunities will arise, not just where the current hype is. This strategic foresight allows for better preparation and positioning to take advantage of these opportunities as they develop, ensuring long-term success and avoiding the pitfalls of temporary trends.

Crafting S.M.A.R.T Career Milestones

After defining your life's mission, analyzing the competitive landscape, and gathering a support network of trusted advisors, it's time to move into actionable career planning. This requires the creation of S.M.A.R.T framework execution blueprints, which will help in manifesting the future you desire through:

Specific: Clearly define the outcomes you want and the decisions you need to make.

Measurable: Establish Key Performance Indicators (KPIs) to monitor your progress.

Achievable: Develop resourcing models to fund your activities.

Relevant + Realistic: Recognize and plan for potential constraints.

Time-bound: Set deadlines to keep yourself accountable.

Begin by breaking down your multi-year vision into manageable 12-week goals or projects. To ensure a balanced approach to life and career, divide your ambitions into four key areas of health:

1. Physical & Mental Wellbeing

2. Spirituality & Knowledge

3. Relationships & Community

4. Career & Financial Building

For each quadrant, identify 2-3 major milestones you aim to achieve in the next 90 days, applying the S.M.A.R.T framework to each. By planning your actions in reverse—starting from the goal and working backward—you can make steady progress towards your long-term vision without feeling overwhelmed by the scale of your ambitions. This methodical approach ensures you maintain faith in your journey, balancing immediate actions with your ultimate objectives.

Case Study Examples:

These case study examples illustrate how to apply the S.M.A.R.T framework across different aspects of life to achieve a holistic balance while pursuing significant goals. Each example demonstrates setting specific, measurable, achievable, relevant, and time-bound objectives that align with the overarching vision for personal and professional growth.

[Personal Wellness Focus]

-Implement a daily mindfulness meditation practice by Q2 to manage career stress.

- Overcome knee inflammation by adopting holistic routines, aiming for recovery by mid Q3.

[Spiritual Knowledge Building]

- Finish reading "Art & Fear" and summarize key learnings on overcoming creative blocks by the end of Q1.

- Strengthen musical knowledge by visiting a global hip-hop history exhibit at the Universal Museum, utilizing backstage connections for an enriched experience by late Q2.

[Relationship Cultivation]

- Organize a memorable event for close collaborators to boost project momentum in mid Q1.

- Arrange a mentoring session with an industry luminary to honor their influence, planned for early Q3.

[Career Enterprise Growth]

- Increase e-commerce sales by 45% through innovative merchandise designs by Q2, hiring a creative strategist for direction.

- Secure financing for a multi-city tour from Branson Cognac by Q3, leveraging their Gen Z marketing support and aligning with a cultural activism mission.

This quadrant approach ensures that while striving for monumental career achievements, individuals also prioritize their well-being and relationships. It's a strategy that promotes a sustainable balance, preventing burnout and fostering long-term satisfaction and success. By organizing goals in this manner, one can effectively navigate the complexities of personal and professional development, achieving a state of bliss through disciplined, mindful progression.

Clarifying Resources & Budgets

With 12-week milestones in place, aligning resources and budgets is crucial to ensure the feasibility of your plans and protect against the risk of underfunding, which could derail your ambitions. Here's how to conduct a thorough financial review to support your goals:

Income Analysis: Start by reviewing your income from the past three years, including both active and passive streams like touring, licensing, and investments. This historical analysis helps identify consistent revenue sources versus sporadic gains, enabling more accurate budgeting and risk minimization.

Expense Analysis: Audit your expenses over the last 24 months, categorizing them into essential and discretionary spending. Understanding your spending patterns is key to forecasting future budgets for scaling projects, launching businesses, or covering living costs, improving the precision of financial planning.

Financial Stability Assessments: After analyzing revenues and expenses, evaluate your liquid assets and project cash flow to determine if you can cover 12-24 months of living expenses, considering the high volatility of music industry income. Maintaining an emergency fund or Financial Freedom Fund as I like to call it, is critical to avoid financial crises, emphasizing the value of a slow and steady approach for enduring success.

Special Project War Chests: For upcoming commercial launches or strategic investments, calculate the capital needed for initiatives like album production, merchandise stock, or marketing efforts. Deciding whether to progress slowly or seek financing for quicker execution involves balancing fiscal prudence with competitive strategy, ensuring flexibility amidst industry changes.

Web 3.0 Fan Funding: Explore innovative funding models like Web 3.0 platforms, where artists can raise capital through supporter investments in fractional ownership tokens. This method offers a modern approach to finance creative projects, leveraging the support of dedicated fans.

Revenue Diversification Analysis: Create pie charts to visualize your current versus ideal income distribution over the next three years, spanning music streaming, touring, brand sponsorships, Web 3.0, and merchandising. Identifying and targeting niche opportunities for income diversification can help stabilize your financial situation against the unpredictability of specific revenue streams.

By meticulously planning and managing your finances, you can navigate the uncertainties of the music industry with confidence, ensuring the sustainability and growth of your career.

Activating Allies & Advisors For Accountability

Without consistent evaluation and realignment, even the most meticulously planned strategies can drift off course, transforming from concrete goals into mere fantasies. Engaging a circle of trusted advisors and allies is crucial for maintaining accountability and ensuring that your vision materializes through concrete milestones.

Here are strategies to effectively utilize your advisors' input to stay on track with your ambitions:

Quarterly Feedback Sessions

Organize regular meetings at the start of each fiscal quarter with both creative mentors and business advisors to review progress. Treat these sessions as opportunities for open, constructive dialogue that can help refine your career strategy and improve your output, focusing on encouragement and constructive advice rather than criticism.

Financial Oversight by Trusted Partners

Work with financial professionals or knowledgeable individuals within your network, such as bookkeepers or accountants, to monitor your income and expenses regularly. This ensures that your finances are in order, funding your plans without unexpected shortfalls that could derail important projects or hinder productivity.

Engagement through Web 3.0 Platforms

Explore the potential of Web 3.0 technologies to create a community-driven governance model for your career. By establishing NFT-based ecosystems, you can grant your most dedicated fans access to provide feedback on your work, participate in decision-making through polls, and engage in deeper conversations about your creative direction. This digital engagement fosters a supportive environment that promotes mutual growth.

Maintaining regular engagement with a network of advisors and supporters across creative, financial, and community fronts helps tighten the execution of your plans. This collaborative approach ensures faster progress toward your goals, keeping you accountable and minimizing the risk of straying from your long-term vision. Embrace the evolution of your vision into a cultural cornerstone that offers significant value to your community.

Overcoming Self-Sabotage & Paralysis

Even with detailed planning, the journey towards realizing your goals can sometimes be derailed by internal barriers. Doubts and self-sabotaging behaviors rooted in past experiences can turn temporary setbacks into long-term hindrances, preventing the achievement of your ambitions. Recognizing and addressing these vulnerabilities is key to regaining momentum and ensuring consistent progress.

Here are effective strategies to overcome self-sabotage:

1) Identify and Address Past Influences

Traumas from early life, negative relationships, and detrimental societal messages can subconsciously foster beliefs that oppose success, holding back career advancement. Techniques such as journaling and somatic healing can help unearth and address these deep-seated narratives, allowing for the development of a mindset that supports your goals.

2) Evaluate Your Social and Professional Networks

Assess the influence of the people around you, especially those who exhibit traits that may undermine your confidence or progress, such as jealousy or negativity. Surrounding yourself with a supportive network that shares a mindset of growth and abundance can enhance collaborative success and safeguard your motivation.

3) Set and Celebrate Incremental Goals

Instead of being daunted by large, long-term objectives, focus on achieving smaller, manageable milestones. This approach helps maintain enthusiasm and a sense of urgency, turning minor achievements into significant victories. Acknowledge and celebrate every step forward, no matter how small, to sustain momentum and build a resilient, marathon-like mentality.

By confronting the underlying issues that fuel self-sabotage, fostering a positive and empowering environment, and concentrating on the cumulative power of small victories, you can dissolve the psychological barriers that impede success. This holistic approach to personal and professional development enables you to transform your original visions into realities, confidently moving towards a future illuminated by your brilliance.

In conclusion, the path to fulfilling your life's visions involves deep self-reflection, guidance from those with experience, and a practical examination of the career landscape. This approach enables the creation of personalized milestones that lead to significant achievements, while also navigating through challenges with the support of a structured accountability network.

However, true success is ultimately defined by maintaining your uniqueness and resisting the external pressures that narrowly judge achievements, overlooking the importance of holistic wellness which is essential for sustained creativity. Prioritize setting qualitative goals that align with your vision before embarking on quantifiable pursuits, which can sometimes detract from the essence of your intended legacy.

Remain true to yourself, crafting a career path that not only advances your aspirations but also uplifts marginalized communities. Shun the limitations of rigid expectations, and with unwavering commitment and strategic planning, embrace the uncertainty that precedes triumph. Continue to move forward with bold perseverance, and let abundance be the reward for your unfettered journey ahead.

CHAPTER 11

SECURING YOUR SQUAD - BUILDING THE TEAM

The wisdom of the African proverb, "If you want to go fast, go alone. If you want to go far, go together," underscores the importance of teamwork in achieving long-term success. For hip-hop artists and entrepreneurs aiming to transform their visions into enduring legacies, building a team of specialists in various fields—creative direction, production, marketing, touring, business operations, and financial planning—is essential. Achieving alignment with these support squads not only accelerates progress but also enhances the journey's overall impact.

This chapter explores strategies for identifying, aligning, and motivating the ideal team to bring hip-hop career dreams to fruition. Through careful selection and collaboration, artists can assemble a crew that complements their ambitions, turning fleeting moments of brilliance into lasting enterprises that benefit communities. By focusing on unity and shared goals, it's possible to unlock a wealth of opportunities and foster abundance. Let's delve into the methods of building and empowering a team dedicated to realizing the potential of hip-hop as a force for positive change, ensuring that the journey towards success is a collective endeavor marked by mutual support and collaborative achievement.

Constructing All Star Teams

Success in the hip-hop industry extends beyond mere talent; it involves the strategic assembly of diverse, multi-disciplinary teams that can distribute workload effectively, allowing artists to elevate their careers sustainably. This approach not only frees up creative bandwidth by reducing the burden of operational tasks but also ensures that progress continues smoothly, even in the face of unexpected challenges.

Master P, a pioneer in the hip-hop world, exemplifies this strategy. He emphasizes the importance of building a strong, multi-generational team equipped with a winning mindset across all aspects of the business, from creative direction to financial planning. This slow, deliberate team-building approach fosters a resilient empire capable of overcoming adversity and creating lasting impact within communities. Unity, according to Master P, is the key to sustained victory.

The goal, then, is not to chase fleeting achievements, like temporary chart-topping hits or momentary social media fame, but to develop a dedicated team that brings a range of expertise to the table. Such a team can navigate shifts in platform trends and audience interests, ensuring that campaigns are not only optimized for current success but are also aligned with long-term community benefits. Through patience and partnership, artists can convert their cultural influence into meaningful, enduring advancements, proving that collective effort and collaboration are indispensable in the journey to lasting success in the hip-hop industry.

Building a Winning Hip-Hop Team Structure

In the entertainment industry, while the allure of solo success often captures the public's imagination, research consistently shows that creative leaders supported by specialized teams achieve significantly greater long-term success compared to those going it alone. The benefits of such collaboration extend across financial stability, mental wellness, and productive output, with teams outperforming individuals by nearly 3 to 1.

This trend is evident in the careers of hip-hop legends like Dr. Dre, Pharrell Williams, and Queen Latifah, who have built extensive networks of experts to support their wide-ranging ambitions in music, film, technology, fashion, and more. Their success underscores the value of assembling a harmonious team of contributors, whose collective efforts transform fleeting fame and momentary brilliance into sustainable, multigenerational legacies.

The key to enduring success in the hip-hop industry, therefore, lies in building dedicated teams that bring diverse expertise to the table. Such teams can navigate the ever-changing landscape of music and media, ensuring that efforts are not only optimized for immediate impact but are also strategically aligned for long-term community benefit. Through patient collaboration and unity, artists can leverage their cultural influence for significant, lasting achievements, proving that the power of partnership is crucial for sustained triumph in the dynamic world of hip-hop.

Within the hip-hop industry, research highlights that the most effective team structures for artists are often divided into two main pods, each focusing on distinct aspects of career development:

1. Creative Business Management

This pod encompasses roles critical for the strategic and financial management of the artist's career, including:

- **Personal Managers**: Oversee career strategy and day-to-day operations.

- **Legal Counsel:** Provide advice on contracts and legal matters.

- **Financial Planning:** Manage finances, investments, and budgeting.

- **Venture Strategy:** Guide new business opportunities and expansions.

2. Marketing Execution

This pod focuses on the promotion and distribution of the artist's work, involving:

- **Digital/Social Media:** Amplify the artist's presence online.

- **Music Distribution:** Ensure music reaches a wide audience across platforms.

- **Public Relations:** Manage the artist's public image and media relations.

- **Brand Partnerships:** Develop strategic partnerships with brands.

- **Web 3.0 Channel Development:** Innovate with new technologies for fan engagement and revenue.

This setup uses specific skills and trusted partnerships to manage both the artistic and business sides of the music industry well. This organized method greatly improves an artist's earnings and influence over time.

Knowing the different roles and how they work together, artists can build their perfect team for lasting success and influence in hip-hop.

Curating High-Impact Teams

Creating teams that last and fulfill hip-hop career goals goes beyond just setting up a team structure. It involves understanding the unique roles within a team, finding the right people through effective methods, and keeping them motivated for a strong, unified group that combines individual strengths to address any weaknesses. This unity is key for building a team that can navigate challenges and form meaningful community ties. Let's look into ways to attract and keep top talent in your team.

Team Role Dynamics in Hip-Hop Success

Successful teams have a mix of different personalities and skills, filling in gaps in knowledge or character as needed. Like a well-oiled relay team where each runner plays a specific role for the best overall outcome, hip-hop career teams also need a balance of specialist strengths and comprehensive harmony.

Here are essential roles for balancing hip-hop career teams, covering both tactical and emotional support needs:

- **The Anchor:** Trusted confidants, often childhood friends or family, who provide personal wisdom and loyalty, keeping the team grounded amidst the chaos.

- **The Navigator:** Experienced industry professionals who use their knowledge and connections to guide the artist's career, avoiding pitfalls and maximizing financial success.

- **The Conscience:** Ethical guides who ensure the team's ambitions benefit the community as a whole, not just individual gains.

- **The Innovator:** Creative minds who push boundaries with fresh ideas and artistic risks, setting new directions away from the norm.

- **The Optimizer:** Practical project managers who turn creative ideas into reality, ensuring plans are organized and goals are met efficiently.

-**The Conductor:** Essential coordinators who manage schedules, travel, and administrative tasks, allowing the team to focus on higher goals without getting bogged down by details.

By identifying and integrating these key personnel into your team, you create a balanced and effective group capable of achieving long-term success and making a significant impact in the hip-hop industry.

United Squad Goals - Motivating and Incentivizing Teams

Understanding what drives your team members is key to maintaining their engagement and loyalty through the ups and downs of a career in the music industry. Drawing inspiration from leadership expert Daniel Pink, author of "Drive: The Surprising Truth About What Motivates Us," we can identify intrinsic motivators that go beyond financial rewards to foster dedication among top talent:

1) Purpose: Motivate your team by aligning with causes that extend beyond just entertainment, such as community improvement projects or educational initiatives. A shared commitment to impactful goals like promoting financial literacy or mentoring young creatives can reignite passion and dedication, especially during challenging times.

2) Mastery: Encourage the development of individual skills and expertise by setting goals that challenge and grow each team member's abilities. Offer opportunities for training, creative problem-solving, and leadership development. This approach not only prevents stagnation but also builds loyalty by making each role more fulfilling and dynamic.

3) Autonomy: Trust your team's expertise by giving them the freedom to make decisions and approach challenges in their own way. Avoid micromanagement, as it can quash creativity and morale. Instead, foster a culture of innovation by encouraging team members to contribute ideas and solutions, valuing their unique insights and approaches.

Creating a work environment that prioritizes purpose, mastery, and autonomy can significantly enhance team loyalty and performance, leading to sustained success. By focusing on these non-monetary incentives, you can build a cohesive and motivated team ready to tackle the challenges of the hip-hop industry together

Establishing Strategic Team Partnerships

Forming effective teams for career growth in the hip-hop industry involves navigating through four primary types of collaboration frameworks. Each model offers a different balance of project demands, budgetary constraints, and control levels, helping to formalize relationships with key contributors effectively:

1. Employee Contracts: Hiring full-time staff on an hourly or salary basis is ideal for roles requiring constant presence, such as finance, legal, IT, and operations. This model offers stability and certain tax advantages but comes with higher overhead costs, necessitating careful financial planning.

2. Independent Contractor Deals: Engaging specialists for specific tasks like publicity, digital marketing, or beat production on a project basis provides budget flexibility and cost control. It's essential to thoroughly vet the quality and reliability of these contractors to ensure project success, with clearly defined expectations from the start.

3. Partnership Equity Alliances: Granting profit-sharing equity stakes to crucial collaborators, such as brand partners or product developers, motivates them to invest in the success of the venture. While this approach aligns interests and boosts accountability, it also dilutes ownership, requiring careful consideration of each partner's long-term compatibility.

4. Informal Reciprocal Relationships: Leveraging informal exchanges of mentorship, opportunities, and resources with industry veterans can fast-track access to valuable insights and networks. Ensuring these arrangements benefit all parties equally is vital to avoid exploitation.

By comprehensively understanding these alliance models, alongside recognizing the importance of team dynamics and motivation, hip-hop artists can craft career strategies that not only elevate their own success but also contribute positively to their communities. The transition from solo efforts to a team-based approach marks a new era in achieving lasting impact and generational legacy in the hip-hop scene.

Enhancing Team Workflow and Efficiency

With a diverse team in place, it's crucial to streamline workflow systems to avoid confusion, duplicated work, or delays caused by unclear decision-making paths. Clear operational processes are essential for maintaining team accountability and ensuring that creative efforts translate into sustained business success and community impact.

Implementing Effective Accountability Measures

Vague responsibilities can lead to a slow decline in team performance. To counter this, it's vital to establish clear accountability systems, including:

-**Oversight Hierarchy & Regular Meetings:** Setting up a structured governance system with regular check-ins (weekly or monthly) helps keep track of progress and address any obstacles promptly. These meetings should foster a supportive environment rather than exert undue control, encouraging open communication and timely adjustments to maintain operational health.

-**Milestone Mapping & KPI Monitoring:** Break down larger projects into manageable stages, using project management tools to monitor progress through daily or weekly KPIs. This approach provides objective insights into team productivity and helps avoid delays by focusing on factual progress rather than placing blame.

-**Clear Role Definitions:** Specify the scope of each team member's role, including their responsibilities, decision-making authority, and required skills. This clarity reduces task overlap and ensures that team members can work effectively without becoming overwhelmed as the venture grows. Keeping each person focused on their area of expertise promotes high-quality output.

By carefully designing workflow systems and accountability measures, hip-hop artists and their teams can achieve operational excellence, turning creative endeavors into successful, long-lasting enterprises that positively affect their communities.

Once a solid system of accountability is in place, teams can collaborate more effectively, achieving goals faster while leaders guide strategy with confidence, supported by clear metrics. The next step is to refine the creative workflow and communication processes to enhance overall efficiency.

Improving Operational and Creative Output

Getting accountability right helps improve how we work, making us more creative and less likely to hit roadblocks. This requires two main steps: making sure leaders make decisions clearly and quickly and using technology to make creative tasks easier.

Streamlining Decision-Making and Authority

For organizations to remain nimble in the face of change, it's essential to clarify leadership decisions and delegation:

-**Delegation Parameters:** Clearly define the division of strategic advice and tactical execution, such as separating the vision for business development from the specifics of marketing campaign execution. This allows teams the freedom to innovate within their areas without being slowed down by decision-making bottlenecks.

- **Issue Escalation SOP:** Establish standard operating procedures for escalating issues, specifying which situations require higher-level approvals. For example, legal agreements might need senior review, while routine social media posts do not, allowing for smoother team operation within pre-defined risk boundaries.

-**Feedback Communication Norms**: Promote regular communication through structured meetings like weekly stand-ups, monthly town halls, and quarterly off-sites. These sessions facilitate updates on progress, discussion of concerns, and team bonding, moving beyond mere task delegation to foster a sense of community and shared purpose.

By clearly defining roles and splitting strategic and tactical responsibilities, projects can move forward more quickly within a framework that empowers both leadership and creativity. This dual focus on clear governance and efficient operations paves the way for accelerated project completion and enhanced team performance.

Streamlining Team Coordination with Digital Tools

In today's digital age, especially with teams often relying on smartphones for coordination, integrating digital tools can significantly enhance collaboration and efficiency, cutting down on confusion. Here's how:

-**Unified Digital Platforms:** Bring together fragmented communication and project management efforts—such as messages, emails, and documents—into one centralized platform. Tools like Asana for project workflows, Airtable for tracking campaign data, and Notion for documentation can create a single source of truth for the team, avoiding information overload and ensuring everyone is on the same page.

- **Automating Routine Tasks:** Set up automation for repetitive tasks like handling merchandise orders, submitting music to playlists, and scheduling social media content. This reduces the chance of mistakes during busy times and lets team members focus on higher-value work.

- **Setting Communication Standards:** Establish clear expectations for how quickly team members should respond to messages, inquiries, and other communications. This helps everyone plan their workday effectively, ensuring time is allocated for deep focus as well as for staying responsive to external requests.

By strategically implementing digital systems, teams can free up time and energy for creative efforts, ensuring that projects move forward smoothly and efficiently. Digital organization and automation support the seamless execution of creative projects, maintaining productivity even as demands and complexities grow.

The Power of Teamwork Over Solo Showmanship

Building successful teams in the hip-hop industry goes beyond just offering good pay. It involves understanding what really keeps a team together, finding the best ways for everyone to work towards common goals, and setting up a system that keeps things running smoothly even when things get tough. The time for going at it alone is over. Now, we're entering the era of teamwork, where groups work harder, faster, stronger, and smarter to bring big dreams to life.

While some may rush for quick fame, risking burnout and getting lost in their own hype, true hip-hop icons know the value of creating a loyal team. By sharing the load, they ensure steady work, growth, and making a lasting impact that goes beyond fleeting popularity.

This exploration of team dynamics, operational strategies, and ways to keep everyone on track shows us new ways forward. It's a call to hip-hop's innovators to unite their teams with a shared focus and drive. By joining forces, your group can achieve remarkable things that weren't possible alone. Now's the time to boldly pursue your unique path, with your supporters by your side, ready to break new ground together. The world can't wait to see the incredible things you and your team will achieve.

CHAPTER 12

OWN YOUR PATH - LAUNCHING THE VENTURE

Walt Disney once said that while you can create amazing things, it's people who turn those dreams into reality. This highlights the journey of making big ideas last, mixing excitement with the careful planning and teamwork needed for success. This final section offers hip-hop creators guidance on making impactful, enduring work by planning carefully, leading strongly, and bringing people together. It's time for us to confidently take charge of our futures, turning our visions into lasting achievements for the next generations.

Guiding Your Strategy in the Early Stages

Rushing into new projects with excitement but without a solid plan can lead to failure. Yale's Henry Mintzberg found that only about 10% of start-ups that rush in without careful planning reach scalability and profitability. It's crucial to map out your strategy and check your resources carefully before you start. Taking your time is key. Let's explore how to successfully approach the market and dodge early pitfalls that could dampen your initial enthusiasm.

Using Stage-Gate Launch Models

Jumping into action without understanding the risks can deplete your resources fast. A smarter approach is to use the "stage-gate methodology," which tests your ideas step by step. This method allows you to check your assumptions against real-world data at each stage of your project, from the initial idea to scaling up, through a series of checkpoints:

1. Ideation

2. Customer Research

3. Prototype Testing

4. Validation

5. Scaling

For instance, when Chance the Rapper was considering releasing his third mixtape "Coloring Book," he didn't just rush into it. He first engaged his fan base with smaller releases and social media teasers to gauge interest and gather feedback. This approach allowed him to validate the demand for his unique sound and approach to distribution before fully committing to the mixtape's launch strategy.

This careful, step-by-step validation helped him not only to manage financial risks but also to build a strong, supportive fan base for his independent music career. Following a similar method can help you make informed decisions, reducing the risk of early-stage missteps.

Performing Financial Reality Checks

In addition to qualitative testing and refining your approach, it's crucial to regularly assess your financial resources and operating budget. This reality check helps adjust your goals to match your financial capacity. Even the most forward-thinking projects need to consider the hard truth of financial constraints, especially when funds deplete quicker than anticipated.

Thinking the market will grow faster or that more users will come quickly can be disappointing if there's not enough money to support it. Making great products usually takes more time than planned, showing that quick success is rare.

Take, for example, the journey of West Coast hip-hop legend Too Short. Early in his career, despite the challenges of releasing albums in the competitive rap scene of the 80s, Too Short didn't rush to produce music just to keep up with the market. Instead, he took stock of his regional limitations and chose to increase his income through live shows, partnering with contemporaries like Ice-T for tours. This approach allowed him to invest in his studio work gradually, laying a foundation for a career that spans over three decades. Too Short's strategy of building his brand and financial base through touring exemplifies how a patient, measured approach can lead to sustained independence and success, avoiding the pitfalls that ensnare others who might seek quicker paths to fame without a solid plan. Patience, as shown here, is more than a virtue; it's a strategic advantage.

Aligning with Partners and Advisors

For launches and sustained leadership to be successful, it's crucial to seek the advice of seasoned professionals who can navigate the industry's inevitable challenges and to form strategic partnerships that boost credibility and open up new opportunities. Success rarely comes from working in isolation without the input and support of external wisdom and resources, making the right alignment essential.

Consider the experience of hip-hop artist Nas. Early in his career, despite his groundbreaking talent and critical acclaim, he faced challenges in expanding his brand beyond music. It wasn't until he aligned himself with experienced industry figures and ventured into strategic partnerships, including engaging with venture capitalists and tech entrepreneurs, that he significantly broadened his influence and financial success. This shift not only revitalized his career but also established him as a prominent figure in entertainment and business. Nas's journey underscores the transformative power of partnering with industry experts and leveraging their insight for career growth and diversification.

Kickstarting with the Right Team

Setting up your venture's initial team is more than just a strategic step; it's about laying the foundation for future success. This means carefully selecting, motivating, and structuring a core group that can handle the early stages of your project, ensuring its survival and growth through the initial challenges.

Leveraging Contract Talent

Utilizing contract talent, especially from within your circle of trusted friends or family, can be an efficient way to manage various necessary tasks without incurring high costs. This strategy allows for a lean operation in the beginning, focusing financial resources on creative endeavors while your initial team manages support roles with a strong sense of commitment. As the project evolves, these early contributors, driven by loyalty and the promise of future rewards, can become invaluable assets to your growing business.

For instance, The Soulquarians were an innovative collective of Black music artists known for their experimental work across neo soul, alternative hip hop, and jazz fusion, among other genres, during the late 1990s and early 2000s. This rotating collective boasted influential members such as D'Angelo, Ahmir "Questlove" Thompson, J Dilla, Erykah Badu, Roy Hargrove, James Poyser, Bilal, Pino Palladino, Q-Tip, Mos Def, Talib Kweli, and Common. Many of these artists had roots in the Native Tongues collective and were inspired by groups like A Tribe Called Quest.

The Soulquarians created a unique sound and approach to music production, frequently collaborating on projects that were recorded during innovative sessions at Electric Lady Studios in New York. These sessions led to the creation of several acclaimed albums, including the Roots' *Things Fall Apart* (1999), D'Angelo's *Voodoo* (2000), Badu's *Mama's Gun* (2000), and Common's *Like Water for Chocolate* (2000), with Questlove often at the helm as the "musical powerhouse." Reflecting on this period, Common highlighted its significance, noting it as a powerfully creative time that might not have been fully appreciated while it was happening.

The Soulquarians exemplified a model of creative and operational collaboration, pooling their diverse talents and resources to support each other's artistic endeavors. By sharing responsibilities and profits, they were able to extend their creative reach and manage tight budgets effectively, setting a precedent for collective success in the music industry. This approach allowed them to maintain their operations and creative output until achieving financial stability, demonstrating the power of collaborative resource management in fostering the growth and success of artistic projects.

Maximizing Growth Through Barter Agreements

Instead of traditional cash payments, negotiating barter arrangements with service providers can be a strategic move for securing essential talent and services without upfront costs. By exchanging services for a stake in future success, both parties can benefit from the growth and prosperity of the project. This method relies on the mutual recognition of value beyond immediate financial compensation.

Master P, a respected figure in hip-hop, often discusses how he traded engineering services for studio equipment or offered shares in his catalogue in exchange for legal advice during the early, budget-conscious days of No Limit Records. He believes that partners who are willing to invest their efforts for future gains show a deeper commitment than those merely looking for quick payment, suggesting that a willingness to share in the risk is a sign of true partnership.

Cultivating an Ownership Mentality for Long-Term Rewards

Encouraging a culture of ownership and sharing in the upside potential with early supporters is crucial for building a loyal and unified team. Offering profit participation and a say in decision-making not only motivates team members through challenging times but also promises significant rewards as the venture succeeds.

For example, during a period of financial instability at Def Jam, committed staff members who agreed to accept reduced salaries were compensated with profit-sharing units. This arrangement not only helped the label manage its budget during tough times but also rewarded these early believers with substantial payouts when Universal Music acquired Def Jam for $120 million.

Such strategic foresight by leaders not only builds loyalty but also strengthens the overall culture, proving that equity and shared success can create lasting bonds and transform collective efforts into significant personal and financial gains.

Crafting a Successful Market Entry Strategy

As we set the stage with clear strategies, aligned budgets, and well-organized teams, the initial steps toward launching tactical campaigns are critical for introducing creative projects effectively to the intended audience. Opting for a gradual, controlled debut, rather than a high-risk, all-at-once launch, provides more stability and adaptability, especially in today's fast-paced digital landscape. This approach prioritizes reaching early supporters first, fostering natural word-of-mouth growth. Let's delve into strategies for fine-tuning market entry while maintaining smart growth and connecting with core fans.

Integrating Diverse Marketing Strategies

Instead of putting all your marketing efforts into one channel, an integrated approach using multiple platforms can significantly enhance visibility and community engagement. By scientifically allocating your budget across various channels, you can engage your niche audience more effectively through repeated, personalized interactions.

For instance, the launch of the innovative music platform Bandcamp utilized a strategic mix of marketing tactics to introduce its services to a wider audience. This included targeted blog posts, partnerships with independent artists for exclusive releases, influencer collaborations on platforms like Instagram and Twitter, and engaging email marketing campaigns. By carefully analyzing the performance of these varied channels, Bandcamp was able to identify the most cost-effective methods for attracting new users, optimizing their marketing spend to maximize return on investment (ROI) before scaling up their efforts. This methodical approach to testing and optimizing their marketing channels enabled Bandcamp to grow its user base efficiently, proving the effectiveness of a diversified marketing strategy in driving successful launches.

Engaging Your Core Community First

Beyond a broad marketing strategy, directly engaging your existing supporters with exclusive offers and early access can significantly amplify your launch. This direct engagement rewards and motivates your base to share their excitement more authentically and effectively than traditional advertising could.

A prime example is Roc Nation's launch of Dusse cognac in 2013, which offered early access to dedicated fans through ticket pre-orders and exclusive tastings. This strategy built anticipation and credibility from the ground up, leveraging genuine endorsements from within the community to create a buzz ahead of wider retail distribution. Such strategies show that genuine fan engagement can be the most powerful marketing tool, especially in the critical early stages of a launch.

Leveraging Influencer Partnerships for Brand Visibility

Partnering with tastemakers and influencers who share content about new launches can significantly boost mainstream awareness and drive sales, as followers often emulate the buying behaviors of those they look up to. The key to success lies in ensuring that these influencers genuinely resonate with the brand, creating authentic endorsements rather than superficial, paid promotions that could harm the brand's credibility.

Take Rihanna's Fenty brand as an example. It strategically collaborated with hip-hop stars Cardi B and Offset, showcasing them in social media posts and select press appearances donning pieces from the AW 2022 collection. This move generated millions of targeted impressions and effectively translated the artists' popularity into tangible sales, enhancing the brand's cultural standing and distinguishing it from mere celebrity hype. This case underscores the importance of context in converting followers into customers.

Maintaining Momentum Post-Launch

The excitement of a launch can capture immediate attention, but long-term success is often the result of steady, incremental progress. Applying the 80/20 principle, where 80% of desired outcomes come from 20% of consistent effort, is crucial for ongoing growth. This section delves into strategies for sustaining growth beyond the initial buzz.

Reinvesting for Continuous Improvement

After the initial success, smart financial planning and reinvesting a portion of earnings into areas like production, marketing, and technology are essential for self-sustaining operations. This approach prevents the volatility of alternating feast and famine periods and supports consistent growth and engagement with your audience.

Expanding Revenue Sources to Stabilize Finances

Depending on a single revenue stream can lead to instability. Diversifying income through various channels and side ventures creates a financial safety net. For example, Jay Z expanded his ventures into different fields beyond music, such as spirits, real estate, and tech, demonstrating financial independence and creative freedom.

Staying Agile with Market Trends

Keeping a close watch on market trends, competitor activity, and audience preferences allows for quick adjustments to maintain a competitive edge. Tools like social sentiment analysis can provide real-time feedback, enabling swift content and strategy pivots to keep up with changing tastes.

Ensuring Operational Reliability

Technical reliability is crucial for sustaining business operations. Implementing data backups, emergency communication protocols, and system redundancies ensures that unforeseen technical issues don't disrupt your business or damage customer trust.

By focusing on continuous improvement, diversifying revenue streams, staying adaptable to market changes, and ensuring technical reliability, creative projects can achieve lasting impact and financial stability. Embracing a long-term view over short-term gains is the key to enduring success in a volatile industry.

In summary, achieving lasting success in the hip-hop industry is a complex endeavor that requires careful planning, strategic risk management, and the assembly of a dedicated team motivated by shared success. Strategic launches and market entry strategies are essential for gaining and maintaining visibility in a sustainable manner.

However, the ability to navigate uncertainty with resilient leadership and constant innovation is what keeps the momentum going, allowing for growth and adaptation as market trends and consumer preferences evolve. Investing in the infrastructure that supports your operation ensures stability through potential challenges.

True greatness in hip-hop goes beyond immediate achievements, drawing on the genre's innovative roots to inspire and guide. By focusing on creating a legacy of artistic freedom and financial stability, and by fostering a sense of unity and purpose within the community, hip-hop artists and entrepreneurs can pave the way for future generations. The time is now to embrace our goals with determination and to embark on this journey with confidence, ready to explore new possibilities and achieve unprecedented success.

CONCLUSION

THE BEAT GOES ON

From its inception at Bronx block parties in 1973, Hip-Hop has evolved from a vibrant form of street expression to a global cultural phenomenon, driving artistic innovation and social change. This genre has not only revolutionized music and entertainment but also empowered marginalized communities by promoting knowledge sharing, creating opportunities for generational wealth, and fostering local entrepreneurship—challenges previously exacerbated by systemic inequalities and exploitation.

As we go beyond the celebration of Hip-Hop's 50th anniversary, it's crucial to reflect on its transformative journey and the impactful legacy it continues to build. This moment serves as a powerful reminder of Hip-Hop's role in challenging the status quo and inspiring a fearless pursuit of creative and economic freedom.

This closing chapter aims to summarize the significant strides made by Hip-Hop culture, identify persistent challenges, and outline a future where equitable support structures enable artists, innovators, and the next generation to flourish financially. The stakes are high, and the time for passive observation has passed. Let's review the progress, acknowledge the hurdles that lie ahead, and embrace the vision for a prosperous future that

Hip-Hop culture envisions and deserves. The beat goes on, pulsating with the promise of empowerment and unity, echoing the resilient spirit of a movement that refuses to be silenced.

Key Learnings - Progress Achieved (We Made It)

The journey of Hip-Hop from its origins in the Bronx to becoming a global powerhouse reflects a remarkable cultural revolution. This evolution, fueled by resilience and creativity in the face of adversity, has made significant strides that deserve recognition. Here, we highlight the achievements and the impact of Hip-Hop over the past 50 years.

Artistic Recognition

The inception of Hip-Hop can be traced back to DJ Kool Herc's innovative "Merry-Go-Round" breakbeat technique in 1973, where he looped instrumental breaks of vinyl records to create a new sound. This pioneering method laid the groundwork for what would become a global movement. Few could have imagined that these beats would one day be part of Olympic ceremonies and Presidential campaigns, inspiring millions worldwide with tracks like Kendrick Lamar's "Alright".

Fifty years on, Hip-Hop has transcended its roots to dominate the pop music scene, celebrated for its authenticity and creative innovation. Grand Wizzard Theodore, another Hip-Hop pioneer, expressed his astonishment at the genre's exponential growth, noting how it has amplified the creative spirit of youth and empowered a new generation of artists. This recognition of Hip-Hop's artistic achievements underscores the genre's significant cultural and social impact, marking its indelible imprint on the global music landscape.

Community Revitalization Through Hip-Hop

Hip-Hop has emerged as a significant catalyst for rejuvenating economically disadvantaged neighborhoods, thanks to its blend of artistic expression and entrepreneurial spirit. Academic studies from institutions like Brown and Cornell Universities have highlighted the genre's remarkable impact, documenting the creation of over 200,000 specialized jobs, the launch of 10,000 companies, and the generation of billions in revenue. These achievements have significantly improved the outlook for areas often neglected due to discriminatory practices such as redlining. Hip-Hop has managed to thrive and build in places left behind by others.

Fostering Generational Wealth

Although the wealth generated by Hip-Hop related enterprises is not as evenly distributed as one might hope, the success stories are nonetheless impressive. Ventures such as Jay-Z's Roc Nation and his involvement in the champagne brand Armand de Brignac and Rihanna's Fenty brands have not only achieved billion-dollar valuations but also underscore the potential of Hip-Hop to translate artistic success into substantial economic gains. These achievements highlight the role of tangible infrastructure in driving meaningful change.

Cultivating Innovation

Hip-Hop continues to lead the way in innovation within the music industry, from its pioneering use of sampling to its dominance in streaming platforms and the exploration of direct creator monetization through tokenization. This forward-thinking approach keeps the genre at the forefront of technological and creative advancements, setting it apart from its predecessors and ensuring its continued relevance and disruption in the music landscape.

Over the past five decades, the architects, advocates, and allies of Hip-Hop have not only championed artistic excellence but have also leveraged it to address socioeconomic challenges in a meaningful way. The enduring resilience and success of Hip-Hop serve as a testament to its power as a force for societal change, proving that art can indeed be transformed into valuable assets that benefit communities directly. A standing ovation is due to everyone who has played a part in this enduring legacy, ensuring its preservation and continued impact. Bravo!

Key Issues Remaining (Where do we go from here?)

Despite Hip-Hop's global acclaim and its pioneers like Kanye and Nicki Minaj becoming household names, significant challenges lurk beneath the surface. These issues primarily affect the vast number of creators who form the backbone of the Hip-Hop community, often overshadowed by the few who achieve mainstream success.

Ownership and Economic Disparities

A critical issue is the concentration of Hip-Hop copyright assets. Nearly 95% of these assets are controlled by just three major record labels, leading to disproportionate profits for corporations at the expense of artists. For instance, Darryl McDaniels of RUN DMC sees only a fraction of the revenue from a catalog generating millions annually, highlighting the stark contrast in ownership and revenue sharing within the industry.

Gender Inequality

Despite the groundbreaking contributions of female Hip-Hop artists, significant gender disparities in leadership roles and pay persist. Women in Hip-Hop, trailblazers like Roxane Shanté and Queen Latifah included, face systemic barriers that limit their recognition and financial rewards compared to their male counterparts.

Knowledge and Financial Literacy Gaps

Many artists and creators lack essential knowledge about rights management, financial planning, and the valuation of their work. This gap has led to lost opportunities for wealth generation, as seen in the case of Hip-Hop photographer Glen E Friedman, who sold his valuable catalog for less than its worth due to inadequate advice.

Web 3.0 and Technological Exclusion

While blockchain and Web 3.0 technologies present new opportunities for artists to control and monetize their work directly, there's a risk of further excluding those without the knowledge or resources to engage with these platforms, exacerbating existing inequalities.

Preserving Hip-Hop's Legacy

As the pioneers of Hip-Hop age, the risk of losing valuable cultural history increases due to the lack of dedicated archives. The preservation of Hip-Hop's legacy is as crucial as its economic and artistic achievements, calling for the establishment of institutions that can safeguard its rich history for future generations.

In conclusion, while Hip-Hop has made remarkable strides in shaping global culture and driving social progress, addressing these key issues is essential for ensuring equitable growth and preserving the genre's integrity. As Hip-Hop enters its next fifty years, the focus must shift towards creating a more inclusive and just industry that honors its roots and empowers every member of its community.

Urgent Calls To Action: Empowering Hip-Hop for a Fair Future

In today's rapidly changing music landscape, where wealth is concentrated and marginalized artists face inequities, it's time to take action. We must modernize the outdated music industry infrastructure and address systemic issues that restrict access to success.

Call 1 - Empowering Artists with Financial Literacy

It's crucial for novice artists to receive comprehensive rights management education to make informed decisions about their careers. By decoding record contracts, understanding rights valuation, planning estates, and exploring cryptocurrency opportunities, artists can avoid squandering their legacies like rap icons of the past. Better decisions lead to better outcomes.

Call 2 - Reforming Copyright Laws

Outdated copyright laws need immediate updating to protect artists' rights while balancing commercialization incentives. We support Congressman Jamaal Bowman's Comprehensive Copyright Reform Bill, which closes loopholes exploited by corporations and ensures fair terms that benefit both artists and creative works.

Call 3 - Fostering Gender Leadership in Hip-Hop

To correct the gender imbalance in leadership positions within Hip-Hop, we must establish specialized accelerator programs that groom promising female founders in areas like label operations, tour/artist management, and content production. Through merit-based succession planning, we can ensure talented women have equal opportunities as current executives retire.

Call 4 - Preserving Living Legends' Legacies

Elder statespeople of Hip-Hop deserve financial security during their retirement years. We propose the establishment of "Living Legends Legacy Funds," supported by streaming royalties and philanthropic contributions from renowned artists. These funds will be governed autonomously by respected culture councils to celebrate the enduring impact of revered hip-hop architects.

Call 5 - Diversifying Public Archives

While the Universal Hip-Hop Museum captures the rich history of East Coast narratives, it's vital to give equal prominence to West Coast and Southern pioneers. By expanding public archives and major institutions like the Smithsonian, we can ensure that the contributions of NWA and other influential artists are properly documented for future generations to appreciate.

The Vision Ahead: Blueprinting Hip-Hop's Empowered Future

By addressing these urgent calls to action, we can guide Hip-Hop into an era of empowerment and equitable access. Drawing from past lessons, we'll unite as a community, harnessing our collective strength to overcome challenges and pave the way for enduring success in the global realm of Hip-Hop.

Together, let's manifest a future where financial literacy empowers artists, copyright laws protect their rights, gender representation thrives, legacies are preserved, and diverse narratives find their rightful place in history. The time to act is now.

Urgent Calls To Action: Empowering Hip-Hop for a Fair Future

In today's rapidly changing music landscape, where wealth is concentrated and marginalized artists face inequities, it's time to take action. We must modernize the outdated music industry infrastructure and address systemic issues that restrict access to success.

Call 1 - Empowering Artists with Financial Literacy

It's crucial for novice artists to receive comprehensive rights management education to make informed decisions about their careers. By decoding record contracts, understanding rights valuation, planning estates, and exploring cryptocurrency opportunities, artists can avoid squandering their legacies like rap icons of the past. Better decisions lead to better outcomes.

Call 2 - Reforming Copyright Laws

Outdated copyright laws need immediate updating to protect artists' rights while balancing commercialization incentives. We support Congressman Jamaal Bowman's Comprehensive Copyright Reform Bill, which closes loopholes exploited by corporations and ensures fair terms that benefit both artists and creative works.

Call 3 - Fostering Gender Leadership in Hip-Hop

To correct the gender imbalance in leadership positions within Hip-Hop, we must establish specialized accelerator programs that groom promising female founders in areas like label operations, tour/artist management, and content production. Through merit-based succession planning, we can ensure talented women have equal opportunities as current executives retire.

Call 4 - Preserving Living Legends' Legacies

Elder statespeople of Hip-Hop deserve financial security during their retirement years. We propose the establishment of "Living Legends Legacy Funds," supported by streaming royalties and philanthropic contributions from renowned artists. These funds will be governed autonomously by respected culture councils to celebrate the enduring impact of revered rap architects.

Call 5 - Diversifying Public Archives

While the Universal Hip-Hop Museum captures the rich history of East Coast narratives, it's vital to give equal prominence to West Coast and Southern pioneers. By expanding public archives and major institutions like the Smithsonian, we can ensure that the contributions of NWA and other influential artists are properly documented for future generations to appreciate.

The Vision Ahead: Blueprinting Hip-Hop's Empowered Future

By addressing these urgent calls to action, we can guide Hip-Hop into an era of empowerment and equitable access. Drawing from past lessons, we'll unite as a community, harnessing our collective strength to overcome challenges and pave the way for enduring success in the global realm of Hip-Hop.

Together, let's manifest a future where financial literacy empowers artists, copyright laws protect their rights, gender representation thrives, legacies are preserved, and diverse narratives find their rightful place in history. The time to act is now.

Manifest with us below:

Vision 1 - Taking Control of Assets

Blockchain technology has revolutionized the way artists and supporters interact, eliminating intermediaries that have long hindered fair commercialization. Transparent smart contracts govern transactions while cryptocurrency enables global citizens to access opportunities previously restricted by traditional barriers.

Imagine trading music rights on tokenized hip-hop exchanges or devoted superfans funding educational scholarships through NFT collections without any gatekeepers standing in the way... Web 3 levels the playing field for all.

Vision 2 - Empowering Gender Equality

As outdated norms crumble in the face of increasing connectivity and transparency, female leaders are breaking through industry barriers, championing diversity and correcting past injustices. The walls are coming down.

By 2030, expect women to manage double-digit billions as label CEOs, directors, lawyers, and decision-makers— a seismic shift from the woeful single-digit ownership percentages that have persisted since the 1980s. Pioneers like Sylvia Robinson fearlessly paved the way for change at Sugar Hill Records, recognizing the evolving commercial landscape.

Vision 3 - Hip-Hop Venture Capitalism

Hip-hop visionaries like Sean Combs, Kanye West, and Kendrick Lamar aren't just entertainers; they've transitioned into billion-dollar investment moguls with serious influence in boardrooms. Through venture capital stewardship and startup acceleration in Web 3 ventures, they fearlessly shape the future.

Culturally attuned venture capital funds strategically invest in frontier startups specializing in direct-to-avatar digital fashion houses, AI conversational lyrics platforms, and immersive concert experiences. Hip-hop's reputation continues to thrive on cutting-edge ideas powered by relentless ambition. No idea is too bold to manifest.

Vision 4 - Triumph of Education Equality

Addressing previous disparities responsibly, underprivileged youth now actively participate in charting their own prosperous futures through universal access to arts education and Web 3 resources. Alumni like Chance The Rapper and Master P revolutionize community engagement, ensuring that historically unsupported generations can code with confidence, produce prolifically, govern ethically, and create abundantly. The world awaits their brilliance.

Vision 5 - Preserving Hip-Hop Heritage

Institutionalizing its roots, iconic sites like Cedar Park in the Bronx and Kool Herc's West Tower Avenue Rec Room are designated as US National Landmarks, preserving their significance alongside architectural legends like Frank Lloyd Wright Halls. Youth from around the globe embark on pilgrimages to these hallowed grounds.

Federal history curriculum also needs to expand to give due recognition to the early hip-hop movement, emphasizing its roots and impact on civil rights and cultural shifts. This approach mirrors the advocacy for broader educational content that includes significant cultural movements and figures, similar to what figures like Congressman Ro Khanna have championed in other contexts, like tech policy, labor rights, and environmental concerns.

By doing so, the curriculum honors a history that has been overlooked or minimized, ensuring that future generations understand the depth and breadth of hip-hop's contributions to society. This commitment to a comprehensive and truthful portrayal of the past ensures that the legacy of hip-hop and its pioneers is preserved and celebrated, marking a step towards immortality for a genre that has transformed global culture. Conscious efforts to spotlight these contributions reinforce the importance of accuracy and inclusion in our historical narratives.

The Beat Goes On... Now For All

As we conclude this momentous 50-year journey exploring hip-hop's remarkable progress in overcoming exploitation and empowering marginalized voices through financial literacy, we must acknowledge that there is still work to be done. We must cement hard-fought freedoms creatively, economically, and politically before complacency leads to societal collapse.

So let us heed the urgent calls-to-action above by rapidly developing equitable infrastructures while envisioning hip-hop's next golden era— one that supports universal accessibility and ownership without ambiguity. Through compassion and capability, strong communities will rise ardently. Now is hip-hop's defining moment as we empower the people sustainably.

Onward we march towards destiny! And in the words of the Honorable Mason Betha better known as Mase, "Can't nobody take [our] pride, can't nobody hold [us] down, oh no [we] got to keep on movin' ♩ ♪ ♫ ♬ ♩ ♪ ♫ ♬ ♩ ♪ ♫ ♬

ABOUT THE AUTHOR

Hi, my name is Ash Exantus, but I'm widely recognized as Ash Cash. I am a leading financial educator, motivational speaker, and the author of over 40 books, with numerous bestsellers that have significantly impacted the lives of many. As the founder and Chief Financial Educator at MindRight Money Management, a financial education and media company, I integrate psychology and personal finance with music, pop culture, and relevant news to enhance money management skills.

Dubbed the Hip-Hop Financial Advisor, I employ a culturally responsive approach in teaching financial literacy, wealth building, and entrepreneurship. My program, Hip-Hoponomics, is particularly close to my heart, where I teach financial literacy and entrepreneurship to high school and college students through the lens of hip-hop.

I am also the creator of the #1 Community for Financial Spirituality, the Abundance Community, where I leverage ancient spiritual texts and universal laws to affirm that Abundance is Your Birthright, guiding members on how to access this abundance immediately.

In addition to my role at MindRight Money Management, I lead BookRich™, a company dedicated to teaching adults, students, and parents how to build a personal brand and become entrepreneurs through creating multiple streams of income from a book about their experiences.

I am the host of a top 100 business podcast called Inside the Vault with Ash Cash, which I dub as the greatest money mindset show on the planet. We interview 6, 7, and 8 figure entrepreneurs and celebrities, taking you "Inside of their Vault (Mind)" on how they became and sustained their wealth. At the time of this writing, Inside the Vault has over 7 million video views, over 1.3 million downloads on audio, and is heard in over 156 countries, including being ranked in the top 100 in 26 of those countries. You can subscribe to Inside the Vault by visiting www.InsideTheVaultTV.com.

Through my work, I've had the privilege of speaking at national conferences across the country, and I've been featured in major media outlets like CNN, The New York Times, The Wall Street Journal, CNBC, Black Enterprise, Essence Magazine, BET, SiriusXM, and iHeartRadio, among others.

Above all, I am known for my unwavering commitment to helping people maximize their full potential by providing the inspiration, tools, and resources needed to live their best lives. For more information on my work and how I can help you, please visit my website at www.IamAshCash.com.

www.ingramcontent.com/pod-product-compliance
Lightning Source LLC
Chambersburg PA
CBHW070133080526
44586CB00015B/1670